THE UNITED STATES AND JAPAN

THE UNITED STATES AND JAPAN: A TROUBLED PARTNERSHIP

by
WILLIAM WATTS

Ballinger Publishing Company
Cambridge, Massachusetts
A Subsidiary of Harper & Row, Publishers, Inc.

International Standard Book Number: 0-88410-993-3

Library of Congress Catalog Card Number: 83-25767

Printed in the United States of America

Library of Congress Cataloging in Publication Data

Watts, William, 1930—
  The United States and Japan.

  "A special study by Potomac Associates"—
Acknowledgements.
  Includes index.
  1. United States—Foreign opinion, Japanese. 2. Japan—Foreign opin-ion, American. 3. United States—Foreign relations—Japan. 4. Japan—Foreign relations—United States. 5. Public opinion—United States. 6. Public opinion—Japan. I. Potomac Associates. II. Title.

E183.8.J3W33   1984   327.73052   83-25767

ISBN 0-88410-993-3

POTOMAC ASSOCIATES

Potomac Associates is a nonpartisan tax-exempt research organization located at The School of Advanced International Studies in Washington, D.C., that seeks to encourage lively inquiry into important issues of public policy. Its purpose is to heighten understanding and improve discourse on significant contemporary problems, national and international, by providing a forum for distinctive points of view.

Members of the board of directors of Potomac Associates are Arthur M. Dubow, chairman; T. Jefferson Coolidge, Jr.; Christian A. Herter, Jr.; Edward P. Morgan; George R. Packard; Timothy Seldes; William Watts; and Mitchell Rogovin, counsel.

This book and its associated research have been made possible by grants from the United States-Japan Foundation, the U.S. Information Agency, and Frederick R. Weisman, whose interest and support are deeply appreciated and warmly acknowledged.

For Bigelow Watts
and
Mildred Lee Watts
in memoriam.

Also for my mother, and
for my cousin and
father-in-law.

Four very special people.

CONTENTS

ACKNOWLEDGEMENTS

The impetus for this book began with talks with Ambassador Richard W. Petree in late 1981 and early 1982. His interest, along with that of his colleagues at the United States - Japan Foundation, Ambassador Angier Biddle Duke, Hironobu Shibuya, and Robert Boettcher, led to funding by that foundation of a special study by Potomac Associates of American attitudes toward Japan, the Japanese people, and the policies of the Japanese government.

Parallel discussions with Gordon Tubbs and James Marshall of the U.S. Information Agency resulted in funding for a corresponding study in Japan that looked at Japanese perceptions of the United States, the American people, and the policies of the U.S. government.

Extensive public opinion surveys were conducted in Japan and the United States in early April 1982, in many cases using the same questions in each study. The result was an unusual glimpse into the thinking on both sides of the Pacific, gathering a sense of understanding and misunderstanding, perception and misperception. These data have been viewed, of course, within the context of other studies carried out over the years by Potomac Associates and other organizations.

As the manuscript was being completed in 1983, an opportunity arose to bring the material up to date. Funding provided by Frederick R. Weisman made possible the repetition in August 1983 of a number of questions asked almost a year and a half earlier.

Field work for these efforts was carried out in the United States by The Gallup Organization of Princeton, New Jersey, and in Japan by The Gallup International affiliate, the Nippon Research Center of Tokyo. Other studies, including surveys conducted by the Shin Joho Center in Japan, have been drawn upon where appropriate.

This survey material provides a rich fund of information on which to base discussion and to draw conclusions and thoughts about the future. But that is only one element of the work. Frequent trips to Japan, intense and rewarding discussions in both countries about the nature of the U.S. - Japan relationship and how our two peoples and governments do or do not get along with each other, and a constant search to understand better the psychology of each side as we try to work out some of the enduring differences between us—these and related efforts have been critical in helping to shape my thinking.

Beyond that, and of primary importance, are all those individuals who have given of their time and special knowledge of Japan and the United States-Japan relationship—whether in personal discussions or at meetings and conferences—to help make this book possible. I hesitate to list them, if only for fear of overlooking any whose names should be included. With apologies in advance to those not mentioned, I would like to express my particular thanks to the following.

On the American side, I am especially grateful to James Abegglen, Robert Angel, James Auer, William Clark, Evelyn Colbert, T. Jefferson Coolidge, Jr., Gerald Curtis, Arthur Dubow, Angier Biddle Duke, Arthur Dornheim, Clifford Forster, Carl Green, Marshall Green, Peter Grilli, U. Alexis Johnson, Arthur Klauser, Robert Immerman, Robert Ingersoll, David MacEachron, Mike Mansfield, James Marshall, James Morley, Charles Morrison, George Packard, Herbert Passin, Hugh Patrick, Richard Petree, Steven Saunders, Robert Scalapino, Albert Seligmann, Isaac Shapiro, Joanna Shelton, Thomas Shoesmith, Richard L. Sneider, Samuel Stratton, William Tanaka, Nathaniel Thayer, Philip Trezise, Gordon Tubbs, Ezra Vogel, John Wheeler, and, others unwittingly left out.

On the Japanese side, I am happy to express my indebtedness to Kazuo Aichi, Tatsuo Arima, Jun Eto, Hiroaki Fujii, Kensaku Hogen, Chihiro Hosoya, Hiroko Ito, Fuji Kamiya, Hiroshi Kamura, Yoshio Karita, Mikio Kato, Ruri Kawashima, Kasumi Kitabatake, Yotaro Kobayashi, Ken Kondo, Michihiko Kunihiro, Kiko Makihara, Minoru Makihara, Yukio Matsuyama, Makoto Momoi, Fumiko Mori, Masashi

Nishihara, Toshiaki Ogasawara, Yoshio Okawara, Saburo Okita, Hiroshi Ota, Kiichi Saeki, Shizuo Saito, Hironobu Shibuya, Kensaku Shirai, Junichiro Suzuki, Yasumasa Tanaka, Toshihiro Tomabechi, Nobuhiko Ushiba, Taizo Watanabe, Tatsuo Yamada, Tadashi Yamamoto, and, again, others unintentionally skipped.

I am also deeply appreciative of the efforts made by a number of individuals who provided valuable technical assistance and help in bringing these pages to completion and subsequent dissemination, including Carol Campbell, Steven Cramer, Susan Crowley, William Diggins, Carol Franco, Edie Fraser, Akira Iriyama, Ian MacKenzie, Marlene Mandelbaum, Robert Runck, Timothy Seldes, Terrence Shorrock, Celeste Wilson, and Leonard Wood.

And finally, I thank my wife Eve for her patience as I disappeared with my KayPro II for hours and days on end. Her understanding made my work a great deal easier.

None of these people can be held in any way responsible for errors of omission or commission. Those are mine alone.

William Watts
1983

1 OVERVIEW
A Look At Some Fundamentals

Somewhere near 1980, relations between Japan and the United States took a marked turn for the worse. As we approach the mid-1980s, Americans and Japanese alike are spending a considerable amount of time blaming each other for the weakening of the bilateral ties that have served us both so very well. What has gone wrong, we ask, and why are supposed friends and partners behaving so badly? What has happened to the sense of cooperation, the mood of give and take, that characterized the way we dealt with each other for so long?

As is usual in cases such as this, there are no quick and easy answers. Many observers say the United States does the larger share of the fingerpointing. Defenders of the American position argue that this is only natural: it is the United States, they say, that bears the brunt of the imbalances that have crept into the relationship.

REALITIES AND PERCEPTIONS

In assessing the foregoing problems, we are dealing with both realities and perceptions. There are, of course, a number of incontrovertible facts—the size of bilateral trade, the composition and balance of that trade, and the existence of security links between the two countries. There are also a number of imponderables—the way that we think about, understand or misunderstand, and perceive each other, and our assessments of the costs and benefits of the relationship.

What follows is an attempt to deal with both sides of this picture, the realities and the perceptions. In dealing with each, it is crucial to keep in mind that our separate images can be quite different, especially as applied to perceptions. If a person, or company leadership, or official negotiating team comes to perceive the other side as unfair, for example, it makes little difference whether that perception is accurate or inaccurate. If the conclusion of unfairness has been reached—whether warranted or not—then that is what counts. Perception, in other words, becomes reality.

Throughout these pages we will be looking at a number of substantive policy areas where there are basic differences between the Japanese and American governments and their respective private sectors. We will also be addressing the murky area of stereotypes and images. We will draw regularly on relevant survey research data to place public attitudes within a more carefully defined context.

Before turning to these points of concern, it may be helpful to take a more comprehensive look at what is happening now, and what has been coming to the surface in recent years, in the U.S. - Japan relationship. A lot *has* been going on of late, with fundamental changes taking place that are affecting our links. Without a clearer understanding of what these changes are, as well of the quite different assessment given them by Americans and Japanese, we run the risk of carrying on a meaningless dialogue. We just won't hear each other.

A Changing Relationship

It is not an overstatement to say that relations between Japan and the United States are in the midst of revolutionary change. In the years following the end of World War II, our bilateral links were marked by a serious imbalance, with the United States in the position not only of conqueror, but also of superior, mentor, and protector. Japan held—and with great equanimity accepted—the position of junior, pupil, and follower. Both sides found the situation reassuring and satisfactory.

In a remarkably short period of time, however, that arrangement has been disrupted. Particularly in the economic arena Japan has made strides that have astonished the entire world. From a position of war-torn devastation, the Japanese people have carried out sustained economic growth that has given them the second most powerful market economy existing today. In the process, Japan has emerged from its secondary position *vis-à-vis* the United States to challenge its former tutor in markets everywhere. According to a study released in January 1983 by the Economic Council, an advisory body to the Japanese government, Japan's per capita gross national product in the year 2000 is expected to reach $21,510, almost two and one-half times the 1980 level of $8,940. By way of contrast, the same study projected the U.S. level at $17,600 in the year 2000, up from $10,420 in 1980.[1]

In many sectors, Japanese products have now become the standard by which people all over the globe judge quality and excellence. It has been a remarkable achievement. The United States, on the other hand, has faltered. Perhaps overly confident because of past successes, and assuming a continuation of American dominance of the global economy, American leadership both public and private simply let things run down, and our position of strength eroded rapidly. The confrontational nature of labor-management relations and the emphasis given to short-term profits and gains resulted in a substantially less competitive American economy, only recently the marvel of mankind. This has been a turnaround, and a shifting of the scales, of huge proportions. Neither side is comfortable with the immediate results.

The New Realities: Problems for Americans

For we in the United States, the Japanese challenge to our preeminence comes as a considerable shock to our national ego. How could these people we defeated on the battlefield so recently have accomplished this resurgence so quickly? There must have been something unfair about it, we say. Furthermore, these spectacular gains—causing great damage to American interests—have been brought about even as we have guaranteed Japan's security at (we are inclined to believe) little direct cost to Japan. The new balance, in which Japan is in many ways America's economic equal or even superior, is hard for many Americans to swallow—including prominent national figures who sometimes vent their frustration and anger at what has happened in terms both unhelpful and unbecoming.

1. See "A Japanese Report Predicts Dominance in G.N.P. by 2000," *The New York Times,* January 18, 1983, p. D8.

That anger is coupled with another awkward challenge to the American psyche—acceptance by the American people, and their leaders, of a diminished role for the United States in the world. That new role, and our attempts to deal with it, have been accompanied by major domestic schisms, culminating most dramatically in the near rupturing of our social fabric over prosecution of the war in Vietnam and Cambodia. It also came as a major shock to witness the drastic erosion in value of the once almighty U.S. dollar, as well as the ability of formerly minor powers to bring our economy virtually to its knees, as happened in the oil crises of the 1970s.

Japan's rapid emergence in the midst of all this as one of the key international actors and a powerful challenger to America's dominant world economic position has added to American uncertainty and loss of confidence in the limitless capacities of our industrial machine.

The New Realities: Problems for Japanese

For Japan, adjustment to the realities of the balance shift has not been all that easy either. Many sensitive observers of the Japanese scene have commented on the preoccupation with order and established hierarchy. Most Japanese are much more comfortable when the lines of authority and seniority are clearly understood.[2]

But this no longer applies in U.S.-Japanese ties, and many Japanese (political and other leaders included) find it extremely difficult to come to terms with the radically changed—and still changing—environment. American criticisms of Japanese performance are frequently seen in Japan as both wide of the mark and unworthy of such a great power. One of the results has been declining respect among many Japanese for what they had come to see as their wise and benevolent older brother.

For the Japanese, other components of these shifts have also been unnerving. Japan is no longer quite so secure and protected, relatively shielded from the vagaries of international competition and pressure. Instead, Japan now finds itself virtually under an international microscope, with more and more demands placed upon it. Japan gropes for a new world role, not altogether sure which way to go, all the while experiencing considerable *angst* in working this undigested reality

2. For a fascinating discussion of this subject, see Chie, Nakane, *Japanese Society,* University of California Press, Berkeley, California, 1970.

through its system. As Japan comes out of the U.S. - dominated bilateralism of the post-World War II period, the natural tendencies of its people to fret and worry find ample sources on which to feed.

The vast changes in the economic sphere, and the instabilities they have introduced, tend to overshadow the fact that comparable shifts in the security and political balance have lagged behind. To be sure, there are clear signs that the tide is turning, but even that reversal brings its own nervousness and uncertainty.

The markedly more outgoing and decisive posture assumed by Yasuhiro Nakasone upon becoming prime minister late in 1982 brought with it heavy criticism in the Japanese press. His whirlwind pace during the first months of office included visits to the Republic of Korea and to the member nations of the Association of Southeast Asian Nations (AS-EAN), Indonesia, Malaysia, the Philippines, Singapore, and Thailand. He made two trips to the United States, where comments during the first visit on Japan's military role triggered a considerable uproar at home, while his relative outspokenness and ability to keep himself in the limelight at the Williamsburg Summit in June 1983 seemed to impress and even dazzle many observers. All this appeared to usher in a new era of Japanese leadership behavior abroad. His avowed commitment to a larger, but still limited, Japanese security role in the region surrounding the home islands also introduced a potentially significant shift.

How lasting these moves and their implications will prove can only be a matter of conjecture. But their very occurence has been important. And the widespread comment and frequent criticism they engendered is an acknowledgment of both their break with the past and apprehension over the accompanying uncertainty that they imply.

JAPAN'S METAMORPHOSIS

The picture that most Americans hold of Japan is, as we shall see over and over again throughout these pages, fundamentally a positive one. It is, to be sure, marked by some negatives, some of which have become more evident over the past few years. It is also probably fair to say that the picture is considerably out of date, with many American images reflecting a reality that has undergone important change. The time lag in these views can be misleading—sometimes dangerously so.

Before we examine in greater detail some of the perceptions Japanese and Americans hold of each other, as well as specifics concerning economic and security ties, it may be helpful to look at some of the differing realities of today's Japan. Much happened in the 1960s and 1970s, and the shifts in social patterns—along with the enduring elements—will have a profound impact on the future of our bilateral ties.

The New and the Foreign Challenge the Old

Throughout much of its history, Japan has been remarkably isolated, shielding itself from outside influence with considerable zeal and effectiveness. Even after the "opening" of Japan in 1853 with the arrival of Commodore Matthew Perry, the Japanese struggled to maintain their separateness—an effort that did not deter them, however, either from adopting much from the outside world or from ultimately embarking on a program of massive territorial expansionism.

Even today, especially in areas removed from the huge metropolitan centers, traditional Japanese ways are passionately protected and respected. One of the factors that enters strongly into the reluctance of many Japanese to see their domestic agricultural market opened fully to foreign imports is their desire to ensure the continuation of the agricultural sector as an integral part of the Japanese way of life. The decline in the numbers of Japanese engaged in agricultural and related pursuits, including forestry and fishing, has been dramatic: from the end of World War II until the present, the proportion has plummeted from about one in two to one in ten, with only about one-third of those working full time.

But as the face of Japan has changed, the intrusion of foreign influences—most of all from the United States—has been enormous. Western clothing styles are now predominant, while Western music, especially rock, has captured the younger market. By now, the near ritualistic "rock'n'roll" dancing in the Harajuku district of Tokyo, not far from the Meiji Shrine, has become a staple for performers and spectators alike. There youngsters twist and spin to 1950s American music that blares forth from their portable stereos, the dancers themselves regularly bedecked in ultramod outfits.

But even in Harajuku the tendency to conform that is so much a part of the Japanese way of life pushes its way to the fore. The groups by and large are segregated by sex, in keeping with the Japanese tendency to keep public displays or even suggestions of intimacy to a minimum. The dancing itself is performed in highly stylized fashion, frequently under the direction of a group leader who blows a whistle to lead each dance step, pattern, or movement. And when the afternoon's activities are over, most of the dancers change back into more staid and conventional dress before moving on to the subway, bus, or other means of transportation to return home. Spontaneity is not central to this semitribal rite.

The Changing Educational Scene

The very existence of the form of cultural expression described above is an important manifestation of the impact of foreign ways. Even more impressive is the extraordinary interest in the learning of foreign languages—especially English. Many leading Japanese dailies print English-language versions. It is increasingly common for the foreign visitor to deliver a lecture in English without the need for Japanese translation, something virtually never possible in reverse in the United States. As one travels about in Japan, it is usual to be approached by students or others who want to practice their English skills. A growing number of publications are printed in both Japanese and English, with the two texts on facing pages, thus encouraging easy study and understanding.

Learning English is a monumental national effort, pursued with typical Japanese efficiency and vigor. It is one that is bound to widen the language proficiency gap between our two countries in the years ahead. This will accrue to Japan a number of important benefits and spin-offs—not the least of which will be direct access by increasing numbers of Japanese to the latest technical journals and associated literature published in English.

American efforts to learn Japanese simply do not compare, although there is recently growing interest in pursuing the mastery of what is, by any lights, a very difficult tongue. Indeed, speaking of the general condition of language training in this country, the President's Commission on Foreign Languages and International Studies (the so-called "Perkins Report," named after its director, Dr. James Perkins, former president of Cornell University) stated that the United States faces

...a serious deterioration in this country's language and research capacity, at a time when an increasingly hazardous international military, political and economic environment is making unprecedented demands on America's resources, intellectual capacity, and public sensitivity.... Nothing less is at issue than the nation's security. At a time when the resurgent forces of nationalism and of ethnic and linguistic consciousness so directly affect global realities, the United States requires far more reliable capacities to communicate with its allies, analyze the behavior of potential adversaries, and earn the trust and sympathies of the uncommitted.

The premium on language study in Japan is, to be sure, yet another reflection of the passionate emphasis on education in that country. By now some 90 percent of all Japanese graduate from high school, substantially higher than the 74 percent who do so in the United States. Forty percent go on to some kind of higher education. Furthermore, Japanese performance standards—especially at the primary and secondary level—exceed American counterparts in many respects, although growing problems related to classroom discipline have recently become a cause of considerable national concern. The emergence of violent behavior, including physical assault and property destruction, has evoked widespread worry about a Japanese "blackboard jungle," a concept alien to the Japanese pattern of orderliness and respect between teacher and pupil.[3]

An Aging Nation

For many Americans and other outside observers, Japan is a country thought to be overpopulated, particularly with young people. So many of the pictures, film strips, and other visual representations of Japan seem to be so jammed with smiling young faces that one gets the impression that much of the population must be under twenty. That is another image becoming rapidly out of date. Consider a few statistics.

As the 1970s began, Japan's population was one of the youngest, if not the youngest, of all the industrialized countries. Even now, only about 9 percent of the Japanese people are over 65 years of age, lower than the 11 percent figure for the United States. (Sweden tops the list, at 14 percent.) But by the end of the century, Japan will have taken over first place, with a prospective 18 percent in the 65 and above category.

3. See, for example, "Japan's Classroom: A Budding 'Blackboard Jungle?'," *The New York Times,* March 29, 1983, p. 2; "Schools Barred 1092 Junior High Students as Delinquents," *The Japan Times Weekly,* June 11, 1983, p. 7.

The total number in that group will reach some 20 million, about double the present count.

In terms of longevity, Japan has already moved to the forefront. Life expectancy is 79.1 years for women, and 73.8 for men. In the United States, the numbers are 78.1 and 70.5, respectively.

The implications of this aging process are considerable. The increasing demand for social services by an ever larger nonproductive segment of the workforce will add to the strains already beginning to show in a slowing economy. This will be accompanied by pressures from another segment of the workforce, the burgeoning ranks of college-educated Japanese, many of whom (as with their American counterparts) are already evincing signs of frustration at their inability to find employment they deem commensurate with their skills and training.

Affluence and Internationalization

In the wake of Japan's astonishing economic achievements have come two developments that are fundamentally changing the way Japanese think about themselves and the way they deal with the world beyond their shores. The average Japanese today is indescribably more affluent than was the case in the early postwar years. Furthermore, Japan's increasing world role is bringing with it a growth of internationalism that is breaking down much of the traditional Japanese reluctance to speak out, particularly among the young. Both factors promote a new assertiveness and self-confidence.

For younger Japanese today—those under 40 years of age, for example—memories of World War II and its anguishing aftermath are at best dim, and for the majority something learned from elders and textbooks. Those Japanese who are now entering the upper middle or senior levels of management and policy making did not go through the wartime experience that marked the lives of their parents. They have grown up in a Japan that has been booming for as long as they can remember. They also missed the unusual relationship that characterized U.S.-Japanese links during the Occupation years, when a special sense of experimentation and nation-building pervaded the atmosphere. Finally, many more of today's rising figures have spent time abroad either in governmental or private capacities, studying, learning, expanding their intellectual horizons, and becoming part of a new breed of internationalists.

It does not require unusual insight to see that these influences are bound to improve Japan's ability to cope with the international environment. Shrugging off some of the earlier insularity and unencumbered with the sense of junior status that was accepted by many of their elders, and at the same time both impressed and elated by the global acclaim that has accompanied Japan's march forward, the generation now poised to assume power and influence should be well-equipped to handle that power and influence. The passionate quest for learning and assimilation of English language skills, noted earlier, can only enhance this prowess.

As an international competitor, in other words, Japan may be an even *more* formidable adversary in the future than she has been to date. That is a potential reality that many Americans, and others as well, are going to find difficult to accept.

LIMITATIONS ON JAPAN

Japan's extraordinary postwar recovery and continued success have been so all-encompassing that they have given the world the impression that there are virtually no limitations on what Japan can do in the future. The national aging process and emergent student unrest and antisocial behavior do hint at problem areas to be reckoned with both now and in years ahead. But the overall impression of something close to Japanese invulnerability remains. Most Japanese would not accept that point of view, however.

Changing Domestic Realities

First and foremost, the Japanese economy is no longer growing at rates that have characterized recent performance. While Americans, and many outside observers of American economic performance, voice concern at huge U.S. budget deficits and their impact on interest rates and economic recovery, it goes all but unnoticed that current Japanese deficits *proportionally* are higher than in America. To be sure, Japan has done a far better job of controlling inflation and unemployment than has the United States (see Table 3-1), for example, but the fact remains that continuing high Japanese budgetary deficits worry many citizens there. Not only that, but Japan now has on its national economic and political agenda a number of major items that are going to introduce or sharpen such internal strains.

Governmental reorganization and administrative reform have been under active debate and consideration for some time. The Japanese bureaucracy is notoriously entrenched and reluctant to accept change. Considerable foot dragging can be expected, as efforts at government restructuring and simplification are pressed forward. This pulling and hauling is bound to have a negative impact on the sense of interaction and consensus management that have played such a highly constructive role in Japan's progress.

Another acutely sensitive issue on the Japanese political agenda is the question of redistricting. As things now stand, Japanese electoral districts are based on land occupancy and distribution patterns that are totally out of date. Something like one-third of the members of the Japanese Diet live in areas that are designated agricultural and rural, even though current reality (the outcome of steady urbanization) would divide that number by as much as ten. One of the results of this, of course, is that agricultural interests command unusually high attention in the political arena—and guarantee that American and other complaints about the closed nature of Japanese agricultural markets find tough sledding among politically conscious Japanese officials, farmers, and labor leaders. Heavy fighting over the process of redistricting can be expected, adding another internally divisive influence.

Further, it is not only the United States that has major industries that are in trouble and out of date. Japan, for example, has been struggling with a sick aluminum industry for some time—indeed, has invested considerable capital aimed at modernization and renovation, only to see negative results. (This aluminum industry experience raises questions about the efficacy of Japanese "industrial targeting," a topic to which we will return in later pages.) The Japanese approach to dealing with the problems of obsolescent industries has been to find ways to phase them out, and this can be assumed to remain the path to be followed. Obviously, this difficult process, at times involving much retraining and redirection of human capital, will add yet another element of tension to the changing economic landscape.

A Skeptical Self-Image

Finally, Japanese have a subtle but nonetheless very real problem with what their self-image. Any frequent visitor to Japan cannot help but be struck by the tendency of many Japanese to see things in a pessimistic light. Professor Yasumasa Tanaka, a Japanese scholar at Gakushuin University who has done considerable research into the sociology of Japanese thought and national character, ascribes this to ingrained Japanese conservatism. It represents, he says, a feeling that optimism, especially hastily drawn optimism—a trait frequently ascribed to Americans, I should note—shows a lack of maturity, good judgment, and common sense. Better to be a bit pessimistic and exhibit caution than to be discommoded by subsequent events.

Whatever the explanation, it is clear that many Japanese do not consider their position in the world anywhere near as strong and secure as most Americans see it. Japan, in the eyes of most of its citizens,

—is geographically isolated from the main lines of global commerce,

—is desperately short of natural resources,

—must satisfy virtually all of its petroleum requirements by imports over long and highly exposed sea lanes,

—has essentially run out of arable land,

—is dependent on a number of industries that are fighting for market share in an intensively competitive international arena,

—is under unremitting foreign (especially American) pressure on a broad range of economic issues,

—is subject to increasing threats from a hostile Soviet Union while far removed from its security guarantor, the United States,

—and more.

Obviously, this is an unnerving self-portrait. To argue with the specifics of the Japanese case is to miss the main point. As we will discuss shortly, the perceptions that Japanese and Americans have of each other—whether accurate or inaccurate—can take on a life of their own. They assume reality.

Geographic Imperatives

To illustrate one final aspect of Japanese insecurity—the nation's physical location—let us consider two examples. The distance from downtown Washington, D.C., to Dulles International Airport in Virginia is approximately the same as that from downtown Seoul, Korea, to the Demilitarized Zone that bisects the Korean peninsula. How would Americans feel if an implacable adversary, one that has made clear its intent to prevail in the end (the USSR, say) were located at that distance from our nation's capital, with borders directly adjoining there, instead of across icy Arctic waters? Suffice it to say that our assessment of our own physical security would be far different than it is now.

To use an example directly related to Japan, suppose that half the U.S. population were packed into a land mass the size of the state of California, and then relocated to the middle of the Pacific Ocean or beyond. How would those inhabitants then view the world around them, placed in a physical reality similar to Japan's?

LIMITATIONS ON THE UNITED STATES

The population of the United States is roughly double that of Japan's, as is its Gross National Product. America's natural resource base is overwhelmingly greater. Under the circumstances, American limitations in the relationship are a bit more difficult to define clearly.

In the very broadest sense, the elaboration of American problems is linked more to sins of omission rather than commission. Obviously, the United States does not face the same kind of geographically induced nervousness as does Japan—a nervousness that has prompted Japan to try to get along as well as possible with everyone without jeopardizing the U.S. security link. Nor, as just noted, are shortages of land and raw materials of anything like the same level of concern in the United States as in Japan.

There are, however, real limitations the United States faces in coping with the very substantial areas of disagreement in its bilateral relationship with Japan. They set the basis for some of our later discussion and are important to touch upon here.

Global Responsibilities

As the international political arena has sorted itself out in the decades since the end of World War II, the United States has assumed leadership of those nations who oppose Soviet expansionism. The costs to the United States have been enormous. Yet those costs have been borne by the American people with remarkable understanding and support. Japan, on the other hand, has adopted (under U.S. prodding during the Occupation, to be sure) a policy of limited, nonoffensive security capabilities. It has sharply restricted defense expenditures, even as its economy has flourished under the protection of the American security umbrella.

Faced with a continuing major buildup of Soviet military forces in Europe and especially in Asia, successive American administrations, clearly supported by public opinion, have looked to their allies to pick up a larger portion of the common security burden. Faced with the need to enhance its naval power in the Persian Gulf area—vital to the protection of those sea lanes crucial for Japan's economic survival—the United States has increased its pressure on Japan to rethink its appropriate defense role.

The U.S. expectation of greater burden-sharing on the part of friends and allies has become particularly strong as the United States has stretched its military capacities increasingly thin and as Soviet strength has continued to grow. This fundamental shift in American thinking is one to which we shall return in greater detail.

The Price of Affluence and Altruism

If Japan has experienced a period of remarkable growth and burgeoning affluence since World War II, the American picture has been even brighter. Especially in terms of personal standards of living, most Americans for many years have become used to a diet of more, more, and more.

Global recession and a crowded agenda of domestic economic and other ills have redrawn the U.S. canvas. The restrictions on life styles these developments have caused for some, and the very serious deprivations they have entailed for many, have evoked both concern and resentment. Where that concern and resentment have been directed externally, they have singled out Japan most of all.

It is important to remember that for many Americans this is not self-pity or scapegoating. It is, rather, a matter of equity. As most of the industrialized world lay prostrate in the summer of 1945, the United

States undertook a responsibility and commitment virtually unknown in human history—to help victors and vanquished alike to rebuild their economic machinery and revitalize their human capacity. Now, less than four decades later, when this donor state finds itself in a weakened condition, many of its citizens believe they are being rewarded by a flooding of their own markets, closed doors elsewhere, and attitudes toward them and their cries of "foul" that frequently border on contempt.

This is a perception, it needs to be stressed, that is held by a significant number of Americans, including many in positions of major power and influence. As such, it cannot be ignored. To the extent that this perception includes Japan as a culprit—and for many it most assuredly does—it clearly is poisoning the well of Japan-American friendship.

Obsolescence in Plant and Management

The failure of the mighty American industrial machine to keep pace with the times is now exacting a heavy toll. As we shall see, the American people themselves can be surprisingly candid in acknowledging these shortcomings. They do not look for a foreign target on which to place *all* the blame, although they certainly are ready to apportion some of it.

What has happened is a process that has taken years. Rapidly rising wages, poor labor-management relations spawning costly strikes and delaying plant modernization, management preoccupation with pleasing stockholders rather than developing market share, an increasing gulf between those who supervise and those who work on the shop floor, national budgetary decisions that have given birth to massive deficits and high interest rates—these and other purely internal factors have helped cause the American economy to falter.

To be sure, there have been external factors at work as well, to which we will turn shortly. But it would be self-delusion not to recognize that a number of short-sighted policies have served to put large segments of the economy in a deep hole. As the body politic now strives to make the dramatic turnaround necessary—a turnaround that some want to see hastened and assured by governmental protectionist intervention—there can be little doubt but that unwelcome pressures will be placed on friends, Japan included.

JAPAN: A U.S. NATIONAL ISSUE

In the space of just a few years, "Japan" has become a growth industry in the United States. It is no longer the private preserve of governmental and industrial specialists, academic experts, or particular geographic or economic interests that had some parochial or special involvement in Japan and things Japanese. In the United States, Japan is now everywhere.

Japan's products crowd market shelves. Its cuisine has become an overnight rage. A television special based on the novel *Shogun,* concerning an earlier Japan that few viewers could understand in any literal sense, drew an enraptured nightly audience of tens of millions. Japanese fashion and art have moved to center stage. One of the leading newsweeklies devoted an entire issue to Japan in all its facets. The "Japanization of America" became the theme for a special series on a major commercial television network. Even devotees of crossword puzzles notice that clues increasingly include Japanese subjects. It all speaks well for American adaptability, accepting the utility and wisdom of learning from Japanese creativity.

As is the case with so much else in the rapidly evolving relationship between the two countries, one must be careful in drawing conclusions about the lasting impact of this powerful fascination with Japan. After all, the bloom went off the Chinese rose in a fairly short period of time following normalization of relations between Washington and Beijing, very much in keeping with earlier historical swings in Sino-American ties.

American expectations of Japan, however, appear to be unusually high—certainly in terms of her material products and accomplishments, but also as a culture and society that Americans appreciate only dimly but about which they show themselves ready to learn. How ironic, for example, that Americans find Japan to be the largest foreign threat to their jobs and yet look to Japanese management and production techniques as something to be admired and emulated!

For some Japanese, this reversal of roles, with Japan the tutor and America the pupil, can have its amusing and even satisfying side. At a recent conference, the luncheon discussion turned to Japan's impact on the United States. One Japanese gentleman noted that this impact can be likened to a popular American television commercial that shows after shave lotion being splashed on a man's drowsy face. Suddenly, a disembodied hand appears in the mirror and gives the shaver an extra hard slap. "Thanks," he says, looking up with surprise combined with gratitude, "I needed that!" Japan, my colleague and his friends noted with smiles of satisfaction, is the one delivering the swat to the somewhat sleepy American economy.

2 DIFFERING PERCEPTIONS

As differences between the United States and Japan command more and more attention, and worry more and more individuals in both countries, it may be useful to look at what one concerned observer said about the state of relations between the two countries some time ago. This historical perspective can be both instructive and alarming, as we consider various alternatives that now lie before us.

Western hope of peace and understanding with Japan is based upon her becoming western-minded and modern-minded, thinking as we do, relating herself to the world as we would. We are positive that we are right.

Japanese hope of peace and understanding with the west is based upon our acknowledgement of Japan's divine mission and acceptance of what Japanese do. Japan is certain that she is right.—In fact, she never has qualms that occasionally trouble us.

The mutual hope of peace and understanding between the two is like that between a husband and wife who have a deep sentimental wish to be considerate of one another and pull together, but whose natures, social conceptions, ideals and aims are so fundamentally different that they drift inevitably towards a break while each, positive that he or she is right, waits for the other 'to change.'

If there is anything to be learned from the survey of a nation's mental growth...it is that Japan will not change. Neither will the west, which feels as justified by logic in its position as a man 'talking reason' with a high-strung woman.[1]

1. Upton Close, *Challenge: Behind the Face of Japan,* (New York, Farrar and Rinehart, Inc., 1934)

These words were written nearly fifty years ago. Yet they must strike any contemporary observer of the U.S.-Japan relationship as remarkably prescient in terms of what we are dealing with today. The two greatest industrial powers on earth struggle to find a satisfactory way of dealing with each other, all the while pointing accusing fingers across the sea. Others nervously watch the spat and await the outcome, their fates dependent upon decisions made in Washington and Tokyo over which their own influence is minimal.

1980: A TURNING POINT?

We noted at the outset that the coming of the 1980s seemed to mark a turning point in the U.S.-Japan relationship. While earlier differences should not be discounted, they did not spill over into the public domain with the harsh rhetoric of the past three or four years. Particularly as Japan has become the focus of so much attention in the United States, the complaints as well as the fascination have become truly national.

That something *has* gone wrong becomes clear when we look at survey responses gathered over the years in both Japan and the United States. They do show a deterioration since 1980 in attitudes of Japanese and Americans toward each other—although the overall balance, it is important to stress, remains clearly on the positive side. While it may be overly dramatic to talk in terms of a crisis in the relationship, the decline is there, it is significant, and it is worrisome.

A NEW MOOD

The increasingly harsh rhetoric has deeply disturbed many people directly involved in U.S.-Japan relations. Nobuhiko Ushiba, former Japanese Ambassador to the United States and one of Japan's most respected statesmen, put it this way in a speech at The Brookings Institution on April 28, 1983:

> It is in Washington that through friendship with many individuals I have developed a profound respect for the United States for its leadership role for the advancement of the free world and the open world trade and monetary systems.
>
> Upon returning here this time, however, I have found in Washington a

new mood that I have never encountered before. I had been reading and hearing about the present atmosphere in Washington back in Tokyo, but, frankly, since my arrival here I have been shocked and dismayed by its intensity and particularly by the resentment expressed against Japan. I believe I am somewhat accustomed to highly political statements flying around in this political capital of this great nation, and yet some of the pronouncements by the leaders of the government, Congress, business, and labor, that I have come across in the past few days go far beyond anything I have heard in my long association with the United States. Washington is not the same Washington I have known over so many years. In that sense, this trip has not been exactly a homecoming and I am somewhat bewildered by the new Washington I have encountered.

Akio Morita, chairman of the Sony Corporation and a highly visible and influential figure in the U.S.-Japan business relationship, made the following comments at a meeting in Washington in February, 1982:

> Instead of treating Japan as a friend, the United States and Europe are ganging up on Japan...treating (us) almost as an enemy....I think Americans are too wrapped up in their own economic difficulties and frustrations to think about the impact of what they are saying and doing to their allies. This is causing a lot of trouble, not just in Japan, but also in Europe, and it is eroding the very fabric of the free world.

Those are very strong words. They emphasize the stress that has entered into U.S.-Japan relations across the board, a stress that has tarnished attitudes on both sides of the Pacific. The solid base is being tested, and it is in the best interests of all who care about the maintenance and improvement of close and productive ties not to let that testing go too far. If the limits are seriously breached, we are talking about an uncertain, insecure, and unstable future.

THE AMERICAN VIEW

Let us turn now to some specifics concerning American feelings about Japan and the Japanese people. As a backdrop, it may be useful first to take a quick look at how Americans tend to think of Asia as a whole, and individual countries within that region.

Asia: Some American Stereotypes

In an extensive study conducted in 1980, investigators selected 15 adjectives or phrases, and asked Americans to apply them first regionally, and then by specific country. These characterizations are, of course, illustrative only, and are meant to represent some of the most common current stereotypes. Table 2–1 shows some of the responses:[2]

Table 2–1.

Asia in General	Percentage of mentions
1. Crowded; too many people	61
2. Underdeveloped	49
3. Political unrest	43
4. Dirty; poor sanitation	38
5. Jungles	14
6. Temples	14
7. Aggressive; warlike	13
8. Industrialized	8
9. Much crime; unsafe	6
10. Peace-loving	4
11. Modern	4
12. Well-educated	3
13. Well-dressed	3
14. High-quality roads, railroads, airlines, and so on	2
15. Many automobiles	2
Don't know/no answer	2

What clearly predominates in the overall views that Americans carry in their heads about Asia is a set of basically negative characteristics: overcrowding, underdevelopment, political unrest, and poor sanitation.

Does this generally unflattering point of view, however realistic or unrealistic it may be, carry over to Japan, or do Americans differentiate? The answer, as the following figures dramatically demonstrate, is that indeed they do differentiate. Japan, along with Australia, stands out from many other nations in the region (see Table 2–2).

2. For fuller discussion of these previous findings, see William Watts, *The United States and Asia: Changing Attitudes and Policies,* (Lexington, Mass.. Lexington Books, 1982).

Table 2–2.

Selected Countries	Percentage of Mentions over 20%
1. Australia	
Modern	45
Peace-loving	45
Industrialized	31
Well-educated	26
Well-dressed	20
Underdeveloped	20
2. China	
Crowded; too many people	76
Underdeveloped	37
Political unrest	22
3. Japan	
Industrialized	50
Crowded	42
Well-educated	38
Modern	30
Many automobiles	23
4. South Korea	
Political unrest	47
Underdeveloped	39
Crowded	33
Dirty; poor sanitation	33
5. USSR	
Aggressive; warlike	57
Industrialized	51
Political unrest	32
Well-educated	21
6. Taiwan	
Crowded	46
Industrialized	29
Underdeveloped	26

There can be little question that Americans do hold some sharply contrasting images of individual countries in Asia, with, one can argue, a considerable degree of accuracy in their choices.

The apparent contradiction in selecting both "underdeveloped" and "industrialized" in the cases of Australia and Taiwan is heavily influenced by education levels: those Americans with a college education said the latter, those with grade school training or less, the former. "Underdeveloped" as applied to South Korea bespeaks an outdated image heavily colored by a "M*A*S*H Syndrome," with the country's highly impressive development submerged by other influences—at once more dominating and less accurate.

But in terms of our principal concern here, the picture of Japan holds up very well. It most certainly is industrialized. Its population density, especially in terms of habitable land, is extremely high. Japan has a compulsive concern with education. In most respects it is as modern as any nation on earth. And there are a lot of automobiles around.

In the very broadest of terms, these findings do not reflect badly on how Americans think of Japan. Whether this equates with anything more than a superficial knowledge and understanding is something we will attempt to deal with elsewhere.

Worrisome Erosion or New Realism?

A continuing series of opinion studies has found American attitudes toward Japan to be consistently and remarkably high—equalling or surpassing those toward a number of countries in Western Europe, and exceeded significantly only by those toward their neighbor to the north, Canada. But that extraordinarily positive picture seemed to reach its peak at the beginning of this decade, as Table 2–3 concerning attitudes toward a few selected nations makes clear.

Table 2–3.

	1976	1979	1980	1982	1983
	(% positive-negative feelings; those with no opinion not included)				
Canada	91-2	92-3	95-2	94-2	91-3
Japan	75-17	82-11	84-12	75-20	71-22
China	20-73	65-25	70-26	66-29	59-34
South Korea	n/a	58-27	59-36	55-40	46-45

There has been a considerable negative shift in the direction of attitudes toward Japan since we entered the 1980s, roughly matching the shifts in views about China and South Korea (starting, to be sure, from a lower base, especially in the case of Korea). The numbers of Americans who expressed positive feelings about Japan dropped by 13 percentage points from 1980 to 1983, accompanied by an increase of those with negative views of 10 percent.

While the balance remains overwhelmingly positive—and this should not be overlooked or underestimated—the negative shift cannot be ignored. It is a worrisome warning signal. At the same time, it may be of very considerable significance that the overall movement in attitudes toward Japan over the past year has been minimal. The drop in positive feelings is just at the margin, in terms of statistical significance, while the increase on the negative side falls below that margin.

Put another way, it is fair to ask whether the negative trend has bottomed out. As we shall see, Americans place a high value on Japan's importance to U.S. interests, and they show concern that the ongoing trade and economic frictions between the two countries will cause serious damage to the overall relationship. Given those feelings, one can speculate that what is now occurring is a firming of public opinion: the relatively sharp drop registered between 1980 and 1982 may have been a decline of those views which were fairly soft in the first place, held by people who were captivated by the initial euphoria of the "Japan boom." Then as the coverage in the mass media of Japan and things Japanese took on a more critical note, and as many public leaders spoke out against perceived Japanese inequities, these Americans tentative in their thinking may have shifted their points of view—thus accounting for the narrowing of the positive-negative balance.

That this narrowing of the gap has eased substantially over the past year may then be important. We may be witnessing a solidification of the public mood. If that conjecture proves accurate, there is some prospect that the ratio of "pro-Japanese" to "anti-Japanese" may remain stable for some time. Such an outcome will also depend heavily on efforts in both countries, both individually and jointly, to put the partnership onto firmer ground.

Positive/Negative Attributes

The percentages noted above refer to overall feelings of like or dislike. They do not differentiate between specifics, but rather lump them together into the prevailing image of the whole. But what do Americans say when asked to mention—spontaneously, and without coaching or seeing a list of alternatives—any two or three things that come to mind about Japan and the Japanese people, both positive and negative? Table 2-4 presents the findings, with only those items or attributes listed that were volunteered by at least 4 percent of the sample (shown in parentheses).

Table 2–4.

Positive Attributes	Negative Attributes
Industrious, hard-working (27%)	Pearl Harbor, World War II (10%)
	Too many imports (8)
Japanese products (9)	Not trustworthy (8)
Technology (9)	Trade limitations (6)
Quality of merchandise (8)	Take away our jobs (5)
Friendly, nice people (8)	Overpopulation (4)
Ingenuity, creativity (6)	Very competitive (4)
Culture, tradition (5)	Car imports (4)
Courteous, polite (4)	Take advantage of the U.S. (4)
Dedicated (4)	

One cannot help be struck by the fact that all but one of the first six items on the positive side of the ledger have economic or material overtones—dramatic reflection of the extent to which Americans tend to equate Japan in their thinking with products and trade. The same is true when it comes to looking at the principal negative thoughts that spring to mind: economically oriented factors dominate the list after mentions of the Japanese attack on Pearl Harbor and World War II.

This shows a mechanistic outlook, one permeated with respect but not much warmth. That hypothesis is supported by a study that tested attitudes of Americans toward a number of countries around the world on the basis of "thermometer ratings."[3] On a centigrade scale, with 50 degrees defined as "neutral," Japan was given an overall reading of only

3. See *American Public Opinion and U.S. Foreign Policy 1983*, pp. 18-19. The Chicago Council on Foreign Relations, 116 South Michigan Ave., Chicago, IL 60603.

53 degrees, barely above the neutral midpoint. That was well below "temperatures" recorded for such countries as Canada (74 degrees), Great Britain (68), France and Mexico (60), and West Germany (59), and also just below both Israel and Italy (55) and Brazil (54).

Character Traits

If one looks at the stereotypes that Americans have of Japanese, the picture becomes more positive (see Table 2–5). When Americans are asked to pick one of two contrasting adjectives that might be used to describe the Japanese people as a whole, they continue to make favorable choices. As in the case of adjectives or phrases relating to Asia, discussed earlier, individual readers may have preferred different pairs of adjectives. These were chosen because they come close to some of the most popular conceptions, or misconceptions, we have of Japan and its people.

Table 2–5.

	1978	1980	1982
Straightforward	50%	64%	53%
Deceitful	37	28	29
Don't know	13	8	18
Loyal	55	70	60
Treacherous	35	23	23
Don't know	10	7	17
Creative	64	72	67
Imitative	26	24	23
Don't know	10	4	10
Peaceful	58	69	63
Warlike	30	25	24
Don't know	12	6	13
Humble	50	66	54
Arrogant	37	29	29
Don't know	13	5	17

Once again, 1980 appears to have marked the high water. In the following two years came a decline—sometimes quite substantial—in the numbers of Americans who chose the more positive adjective, bringing the overall shape of favorable views more in line with those held in 1978. Unlike the corresponding increase in overall negative opinions on the like/dislike scale noted in the preceding section, however, the proportions of Americans who selected the negative character trait remained virtually unchanged between 1980 and 1982, with levels in both years considerably below those held in 1978.

The drop on the positive side is accounted for by larger percentages in 1982 who expressed no opinion. What lies behind that shift in terms of current reality is open to speculation, with a number of factors assuredly at work. One, of course, is the major increase in media reporting on Japan that has taken place in recent years. That jump in quantity (although not always quality) has tended to focus on the negatives in the relationship, especially as they relate to economic items. These, in turn, can have direct impact on individual Americans, who have come to see Japan as a serious threat to American jobs. (This is discussed further in Chapter 4.)

Not only has media reporting on Japan surged upwards, but so has Japan's general presence in the United States. It is now everywhere, and highly visible. Its goods are big-ticket items, not less recognizable products such as shirts or some kinds of athletic equipment. This only adds to the threat image, as well as making more pertinent the widely reported American complaints about gaining market access in Japan.

Under such pressures, the positive image that Americans have of Japanese personal traits has declined. The effect has not been enough, as yet, to translate into a corresponding increase in the negative.

It is useful to point out once again that the balance in all cases is clearly on the positive side. Not only that, but, as was found in 1980, Japanese also rank comparatively well when put up against other peoples in the region in this personality test (see Table 2–6).

While Australians generally receive more favorable marks on character traits than do Japanese (especially in the very low percentages given to Australians in terms of being "warlike," "treacherous," or "deceitful"), the margins in some cases are small. Given the widespread American identification of Australia with Great Britain and our own cultural and historical heritage, one can argue that these responses

Table 2–6.

	Japan	China	USSR	Australia
Straightforward	64%	55%	26%	86%
Deceitful	28	37	67	4
Don't know	8	8	7	10
Loyal	70	60	36	86
Treacherous	23	33	58	5
Don't know	7	7	6	9
Creative	72	55	39	67
Imitative	24	39	54	23
Don't know	4	6	7	10
Peaceful	69	55	22	89
Warlike	25	39	72	3
Don't know	6	6	6	8
Humble	66	63	24	66
Arrogant	29	31	69	23
Don't know	5	6	7	11

reflect remarkably well on Japan. And surely the considerable preference shown for Japanese over Chinese and overwhelmingly over Russians ("people of the Soviet Union," in the 1980 survey wording) is striking. The post-recognition excitement of Americans about China and things Chinese has not led to displacement of Japanese by Chinese in this opinion measurement.

Today and Tomorrow: An Assessment

Clearly, the general perceptions that Americans have of Japan and the Japanese people are marked by many positive features. Industrious, creative, makers of high-quality products, and—if one can judge from the burst of interest in Japanese fashion and, especially, food (witness the proliferation across the United States of *sushi* bars and restaurants) —increasingly the target of interest from a more cultural/humanistic point of view, Japanese have entered the American way of life in an important and enduring manner.

But this entrance, encouraging and important as it may be, is not without its problematic side. And when the picture is viewed in its least focussed state, the downward swing becomes more prominent. This is the necessary conclusion that must be drawn from Table 2-7, which shows responses to a very broad question posed over the years concerning the state of current relations.

Table 2-7.

State of Current Relations As Seen by Americans	1978 %	1982 %	1983 %
Excellent	8	6	6
Good	52	43	38
Only fair	28	39	39
Poor	3	6	8
Don't know	9	6	9

If the numbers of those who gave the positive answers ("excellent" and "good") are grouped, and contrasted with the negatives ("only fair" and "poor"), the negative trend is striking. What had been a ratio of 60 - 31 percent on the affirmative side in 1978—a margin of close to two-to-one—had given way four years later to a small positive plurality of 49 - 45 percent. And by late summer of 1983, the plurality had actually fallen into the negative column—44 - 47 percent.

At the same time, one can also argue that this shift shows an increasing awareness on the part of Americans of the difficulties now surrounding bilateral U.S.-Japan ties. In this sense, the more somber reading of the state of current relations can be viewed as a step toward realism. Such a more realistic awareness of the problems can be, after all, a sign of maturity in thinking about how and where things stand.

The downward slippage in the views of Americans is repeated in Table 2-8 when we look at comparative assessments about what the future is likely to hold:

Table 2-8.

Future Relations Are More Likely To:	1978 (%)	1982 (%)
Get better	21	23
Get worse	14	23
Stay about the same	54	46
Don't know	11	8

In this measurement, close to half of the American people in the most recent testing expected things to stay about the same as they looked ahead, with the remainder split evenly between those who thought things would get better and those who thought things would get worse. This is another decline from earlier findings: the numbers who see a future downturn were higher in 1982 than four years earlier, paralleling a similar drop in the numbers who foresaw little future change.

THE JAPANESE VIEW

As discussed later when we deal with the specifics of economic and security-related issues, Japanese thinking about the United States can also have its rough spots. Basically positive overall, Japanese opinion shows areas of softness and weakened confidence in America. Such concern can be expressed at times in terms both anguished and exasperated, as we saw above in the comments of Messrs. Ushiba and Morita.

In the decades immediately following World War II, the sense that America was in many areas all-powerful and all-wise pervaded Japanese thinking. The Occupation, for some of its harsher and even seamier sides, brought with it very large doses of generosity and understanding from victor toward vanquished. The Japanese acceptance of *amae,* or a dependent relationship between superior (the United States) and inferior (Japan), proved particularly appropriate for this period.

The United States: Feet of Clay?

Today, especially among younger Japanese, a different and more assertive appreciation of U.S.-Japan links is coming to the fore. Perhaps nothing has dramatized this more forcefully in a personal way than an experience that occurred to the author during a visit to Japan in early 1983.

> One of the pleasantest episodes in my regular trips to Japan is an evening spent with two of my closest Japanese friends. Each time, they invite me to their home for a small informal dinner, at which they regularly include one or two younger employees of the major trading company where my host holds a prominent and highly challenging position. Over the years, I have observed a subtle yet profound change in the way these junior partners

(different on each occasion) have handled themselves—especially with the visiting *gaijin*. The shift has been steady, with increasing self-confidence very much in evidence.

During the early-1983 dinner, our discussion focused for a good portion of the evening on how Japanese felt about the many American pressures for more defense spending, greater market access, elimination of nontariff barriers, and the like—standard fare for many such friendly yet serious social occasions. As the dialogue progressed, I raised the theme of anti-Americanism, actual or potential. Is there not the likelihood that these constant pressures will irritate and ultimately alienate great numbers of Japanese? Is it already happening, and, if not, will it? The response from one of the younger guests was, to me at least, most revealing. "It's not anti-Americanism in any 'Yankee go home' sense," he said. "We feel sorry for you."

The image of the United States with which he and his generation had grown up, he went on to say, was one totally imbued with strength, leadership, dynamism, and indestructible optimism. All Japanese had been taught to admire and respect this colossus across the ocean, mighty in victory and even mightier in its graciousness and sensitivity in managing that victory. Japan, he and his generation were taught to believe, was fortunate indeed to have such a friend, and could learn much from this benefactor.

"But what has happened to you?," he went on to ask. Now this great nation of power and wisdom seems to have lost faith in itself. Instead of being a leader, it is constantly on the lookout to find ways to blame its internal weaknesses and failings on others—most of all Japan, which had followed the precepts of its former adversary and had done everything within its own capabilities to prove itself an exemplary student.

This was heady stuff, and not something heard much before—especially from a junior employee in the home of his superior, talking to that host's guest of honor. To be sure, there was much discussion of whether the pupil had learned too well, had broken the rules of the game, and thereby had provoked justifiably his preceptor's concern and even wrath. But in one very important sense, that was not the real point. Feeling sorry may be near to something far more disconcerting than pity: contempt.

A Historic Irony

As a child growing up in New York in the 1930s, I recall the frequent condescending remarks about Japan as "the country that makes toys that break." For too long, we Americans lived with an unrealistic and frequently contemptuous view of Japan and its people. During World War II, that turned to dislike, at times tinged with hysteria. The extraordinary turnabout in those views in recent years, as exemplified by so many of the attitudes implicit in the survey findings reported in this book, is a tribute to Japan's astonishing postwar development and American acknowledgment of that fact.

As the magnitude of their own domestic achievement becomes firmly rooted within the Japanese psyche, and as the Japanese people begin to wonder about the will and staying power of their protector and tutor, what a quirk of history it would be if the earlier American condescension—even contempt—were to be reciprocated from the opposite direction.

A study published in June 1983 suggests that such may already be coming to pass among some Japanese. Citizens surveyed by The Gallup Organization for *Newsweek* magazine in Japan, France, West Germany, Great Britain, Brazil, and Mexico were given a number of personality traits applicable to Americans from which they were asked to choose. Those most often selected by Japanese were "nationalistic," "friendly," "decisive," "rude," and "self-indulgent." Those least associated with Americans, according to Japanese respondents, were "industrious," "lazy," "honest," and "sexy." In looking at the overall characterizations picked by representatives of the other countries in this particular survey, it is fair to say that the least flattering picture of Americans was the one held by Japanese.

America: How Trustworthy?

In a later discussion of defense and security matters, we will see that Japanese are considerably less confident about the readiness of the United States to come to their defense if threatened by Soviet attack than are Americans to express such a commitment (see Chapter 5).

This uncertainty finds a parallel in the steady decline since 1980 in assessments of the trustworthiness of the United States. As reported in late November, 1982, in the *Yomiuri Shimbun,* Japan's largest circulation daily, together with comparable earlier *Yomiuri* reports, the Japanese sense of American trustworthiness has been shaken, as Table 2–9 makes clear.

Table 2–9.

Listed below are the names of 30 nations. Which five do you regard as especially trustworthy? (Only the ten most popular countries are included here.)

	1978 (%)	1979 (%)	1980 (%)	1981 (%)	1982 (%)
1. United States	41	46	59	56	50
2. Great Britain	23	28	35	33	35
3. China	24	28	38	35	31
4. Switzerland	21	24	25	27	29
5. France	15	23	23	24	28
6. Canada	20	23	27	25	25
7. West Germany	20	22	25	27	25
8. Australia	14	17	21	19	20
9. Brazil	18	18	17	16	15
10. Netherlands	5	8	6	9	11

While the United States remains the single most trustworthy nation in the eyes of the Japanese people, the erosion in that trust since 1980 was significant. By 1982 not quite one Japanese in two (49.6 percent in the unrounded results) put the United States in the "especially trustworthy" category—a drop of nine points in two years. Only China suffered a comparable loss in the ratings over this period, undoubtedly a reflection of the widespread disappointment in Japan over failed hopes in economic relations.

The U.S. decline stems, we can safely assume, from some of the factors inherent in the "we are sorry for you" sentiment. The sense of constant buffeting from America and Americans that more and more Japanese are coming to feel, combined with their perception of American economic weaknesses and failures, have forced many Japanese to reassess the trustworthiness of their largest trading partner and sole military ally.

That same *Yomiuri* survey also reported views over time about the health of U.S.-Japan bilateral relations (see Table 2–10).

Table 2–10.

Would you say that relations between the United States and Japan are good at present, or not?

	1978 (%)	1979 (%)	1980 (%)	1981 (%)	1982 (%)
Very good	2	3	4	3	2
Good	41	44	45	40	32
Neither good nor bad	32	32	28	32	35
Bad	10	12	13	15	22
No answer	15	9	10	10	9

If we collapse these responses into positive, neutral, and negative groups, we find the results in Table 2–11.

Table 2–11.

	1978	1979	1980	1981	1982
Positive	43	47	49	43	34
Neutral	32	32	28	32	35
Negative	10	12	13	15	22
(Positive/negative balance	(+33)	(+35)	(+36)	(+28)	(+12)

A switch of significant and disturbing proportions has taken place. From the high point in 1980, the balance once again has been badly frayed. A very substantial positive ratio has been sharply reduced, dropping 24 points in just two years.

These *Yomiuri* findings are strikingly close to similar measurements in the 1982 and 1983 binational studies reported throughout these pages. Those results concerning Japanese views on the current relationship, juxtaposed with what was recorded from American eyes as reported above, are shown in Table 2–12.

Table 2–12.

Current Relations	1982		1983	
	US	Japan	US	Japan
Excellent	6%	2%	6%	2%
Good	43	22	38	19
Only fair	39	39	39	42
Poor	6	19	8	14
Don't know	6	18	9	23

These figures showed, in 1982, a bare plurality of Americans on the positive side (49-45 percent), but an impressive majority of Japanese of a negative frame of mind (58-24 percent). By 1983, the Japanese majority had been joined by an American plurality—47-44 percent on the negative side of the equation.

The American ambivalence and Japanese pessimism are mirrored, furthermore, in their comparative views of the future, as registered in 1982 and displayed in Table 2–13.

Table 2–13.

Future Relations Will:	U.S.	Japan
Get better	23%	3%
Get worse	23	21
Stay about the same	46	48
Don't know	8	28

Among Americans, close to half the populace expects things to stay about the same; the remainder split evenly between optimists and pessimists.

For Japanese, the number of those who choose the middle and safer ground is about the same as in the United States, as is the proportion that foresees darker days ahead. But only about one Japanese in thirty expresses a belief that relations will improve, surely a cautious assessment.

3 ECONOMIC RELATIONS
Overview and Complaints

By now it has become a truism to say that economic relations between the United States and Japan are crucial for the well-being of both partners, as well as for the global economy as a whole. A truism perhaps, but also a fact of such fundamental importance that we take it for granted at our own risk. Just as in the case of defense and security links between Tokyo and Washington, it is worth reminding ourselves with some regularity of what the impact would be on each economy, and those of suppliers and purchasers, wherever located, if the massive productive and exchange system now in place were to rupture under the blows of trading wars, protectionism, internal bickering, or some other divisive force. The beneficiaries of that development, whether friend or foe, would be few.

AN OVERVIEW

The United States is Japan's largest trading partner; Japan ranks second only to Canada as a U.S. trading partner. Two-way U.S. - Japanese trade in 1982 surpassed $60 billion. Two-way investment between the two nations is more than $13 billion. Japan's imports of U.S. agricultural products—some $7 billion worth—amount to 15 percent of U.S. exports, close to twice the proportion of any other country. Nearly one-fourth of all automobiles sold in the United States are Japanese made. The list of products, supplies, and technology for which the two depend on each other is large and growing.

Behind this growth—all the more remarkable considering the speed with which it has occurred—there lurks the variety of complaints and frictions that have come to dominate U.S.-Japan trade and economic intercourse. Japan's enormous presence in the United States has created serious image problems of its own. As Japan has taken a larger place in the U.S. market, and as its visibility has enlarged dramatically, Americans look at the surging trade imbalance between the two (some $17 billion in favor of Japan in 1982 and growing steadily) and find themselves discomfited by this rapid change in fortune. Charges of "unfair" fly back and forth across the Pacific, injecting recrimination into the bilateral dialogue. (Between Japan and many European countries, it should be noted, the recriminations are often much sharper.)

These charges are supported in the eyes of American critics by what is seen as Japan's considerably better economic performance. This better performance makes it incumbent upon Japan, they believe, to be more forthcoming in its efforts to ease international economic strains, especially the corrosive difficulties between Japan and the United States.

In this regard, consider, for example, some comparative performance figures in Table 3-1 for 1982 among the "Big Seven," the regular economic summit participants:[1]

Table 3-1.

	Unemploy-ment rate (in %)	Infla-tion (in %)	Capacity utilization in mfg (in %)	Balance of pay-ments ($US billions)
Britain	12.0	8.6	78	+6.80
Canada	11.1	10.7	67	+2.15
France	8.6	12.0	78	−12.37
Italy	9.1	16.4	71	−5.65
Japan	2.4	2.6	85	+7.28
U.S.	9.6	6.2	70	−8.09
Germany	7.7	5.3	77	+3.22

1. *The New York Times,* May 29, 1983, Section 4, page 1.

Japan's superior record—lowest rates of unemployment and infla-tion, highest level of plant capacity utilization, and largest balance of payments surplus—generates pressure on her to "do more," with differ-ent ideas as to what that "more" should be.

COMPLAINTS: THE AMERICAN VIEW

From the American standpoint, some of the key complaints can be summarized as follows:

1. The Japanese market remains, in many areas, either closed or highly restricted. In a major speech delivered in December 1982, American Ambassador to Japan Mike Mansfield described the situation this way:

> ...it is clear that Japanese exports to the United States have achieved significant penetration of the U.S. market in many areas while the U.S. share of the Japanese market in areas where we should be most competitive is strikingly low. In addition to Japan's nearly one-quarter share of the U.S. auto market, many other Japanese products now hold major shares of the U.S. market. To illustrate my point, last year's (1981) figures indicate that in steel Japan held a 10 to 15 percent share of the U.S. market; in TVs, 20 to 30 percent; in motorcycles, 90 percent; in radios, 50 to 60 percent; in cameras, over 30 percent; in recording equipment, over 50 percent; in watches, over 50 percent; and, in machine tools, over 20 percent. By contrast, representa-tive competitive U.S. products hold only the following limited share of the market in Japan—cigarettes, 1.3 percent in comparison to more than a 50 percent share of cigarette sales in Hong Kong, a market very similar to Japan's; communications equipment, 1.3 percent; fresh oranges, 3 percent; medical equipment, 6.3 percent; office automation equipment, 11.2 percent; beef, 7 percent; as well as unreasonably low market shares for such competitive products as analytical instruments, wood products, industrial chemicals, and pharmaceuticals.[2]

Coming from an American envoy who is widely regarded as both an outstanding diplomat and a wise but also sympathetic observer of the Japanese scene, these figures, and the problem they represent, deserve careful attention.

2. Speech before the Yomiuri International Economic Society, delivered at Keidanren Hall, Tokyo, December 9, 1982; see "Speaking of Japan," April 1983, Keizai Koho Center, Japan Institute for Social and Economic Affairs, Tokyo, Japan. It might be noted that the reference to U.S. market share of Hong Kong's cigarette sales does not take note of the fact that Hong Kong, unlike Japan, does not have a major tobacco industry of its own.

2. While Japan has come a long way in dealing with some aspects of its closed market, the barriers that remain are real and serious—although in many areas they are difficult to quantify and prove. Lengthy and difficult licensing and inspection procedures have drawn much fire, although steps announced in the spring of 1983 gave hope that some of these troublesome impediments might be eased and, hopefully, removed. Frequent complaints are also heard about the intricate and outdated Japanese distribution system, as well as a "buy Japanese" mentality—both of which work against foreign imports.

3. Given the enormous trade imbalance between the two countries, many American critics (including some of the most vociferous and most influential on Capitol Hill) argue that Japan should act on its own to meet the complaints and pressures from various external quarters. Japan's perceived reluctance to take necessary steps, or to do so only in the face of such foreign pressures—and grudgingly at that—add to the sense of annoyance and frustration in the United States and elsewhere.

4. More recently, Japan has been accused of "industrial targeting," or developing national policies that favor certain industries in Japan by giving them special tax and investment support, protective advantages, and cartel-like opportunities that provide a tremendous leg up against foreign competition. In this regard, the Ministry of International Trade and Industry (MITI) is viewed with particular suspicion, seen as an ominous and extraordinarily powerful agency that pulls strings and gives virtually binding guidance to vast sectors of Japanese industry — with results that are criticized as unfair, and apparently little short of miraculous.

Such alleged interweaving of governmental influence with industrial policy has strengthened concern about the colossus called "Japan Inc." While the merits of these arguments have remained open to discussion, by mid-1983 this had become one of the most contentious issues in the U.S.-Japan economic dialogue.

5. For some outside observers, a further source of major complaint has been the undervaluation of the Japanese yen against the U.S. dollar. This considerable deviation from realistic relative strengths of the two currencies has artificially inflated the price of American goods, making

3. See, for example, "Industrial Policy Is Not the Major Reason for Japan's Success," by Philip H. Tresize, *The Brookings Review,* Spring 1983, pp. 13-18.

them all the harder to sell in Japan, even as it has had precisely the opposite effect where Japanese goods entering the U.S. market are concerned.

A prominently featured newspaper article, carried on the day the May 1983 Williamsburg economic summit got fully under way, described the situation in these terms:

> The connection between trade and foreign exchange rates is straightforward. Most foreign trade is conducted in dollars. When the yen goes down in value it means a Japanese car company can charge Americans fewer dollars and still collect as many yen as before when it converts the dollars back into its own currency.
>
> This is what has been happening to U.S. industry.
>
> Consider, for example, the tribulations of Caterpillar, the largest U.S. manufacturer of earth moving equipment. In the first part of 1982, when the yen was trading at between 230 and 260 to the dollar, Caterpillar steadily lost sales to its leading competitor, Japan's Komatsu. Caterpillar's overseas sales fell by 14 percent in the first half of the year, while Komatsu's rose by almost 50 percent. Caterpillar won't become competitive again until the yen gets stronger.
>
> It is the same in cars and computer chips. If the yen is undervalued by 20 percent, as many experts think it is, then Japanese automakers can keep the dollar price of their cars about $1500 less than it would be in a fairer world—or they can keep prices higher and reap a windfall.
>
> These distortions have little to do with the relative efficiency of Japanese and U.S. industry. Instead they are produced by an international financial system that works better for speculators and financial managers than for the producers of goods.[4]

This story, repeated almost endlessly by injured and angered American corporate leaders, has become central to the U.S. - Japan economic dialogue. And when its effects are viewed within the framework of Japan's strong economic performance, as the comparative figures cited above demonstrate, then the psychological and political impact is made all the more powerful.

This is a formidable list of complaints. As we shall see, it is matched by Japan's own list of grievances. Taken together, they represent an imposing challenge to smooth economic and trade ties between our two countries.

4. "Americans Unite! To Achieve Prosperity Buy Japanese Money," by Dan Morgan, *The Washington Post*, May 29, 1983, page C1.

COMPLAINTS: THE JAPANESE VIEW

He who lives in a glass house should not throw stones. While there are, to be sure, areas of the Japanese economy that are given special protection, the same holds true in the United States; segments of the American agricultural industry, for example, are shielded from foreign competition, as are other sectors that are in trouble and which Americans do not wish to see wiped out. Such a concern for the maintenance of Japan's declining agricultural base is one that outsiders should be able to understand. Japan does not wish to see that part of its traditional economy and life style eradicated, nor does it wish to see its national security in this sector subject to the threat of total dependence on imports that already prevails for oil and petroleum products, for example. Certain political realities should be acceptable to both sides in such disputes.

The same reasoning applies to American charges of industrial targeting by Japan. How can the United States raise such a fuss about this issue, ask many Japanese, when the United States is doing the same thing? The Japanese position was well stated by one observer as follows:

It is rarely good negotiating practice to deny the obvious, and it is particularly foolish to maintain...that the U.S. government is not deliberately and vigorously supporting the development of the American computer industry. ...in Washington, there is very little hesitation among officials at the Defense Department, NASA, the Energy Department, or the National Science Foundation to talk about that interesting subject.

The indictment of Japanese industrial policy in its most sweeping form— by American machine tool makers, for example—charges that it involves cartelized research and development with direct financial support for private companies from the government. Meanwhile, a dozen American microchip manufacturers have obtained a conditional antitrust waiver from the Justice Department and are organizing joint research through the new Microelectronics and Computer Technology Corporation (MCTC). As for financial support, the U.S. Defense Department alone intends to put as much money into advanced computers over the next several years as the Japanese government is allocating for its fifth-generation computer project....

Since American government agencies are actively working to maintain the superiority of American technology in crucial fields, it is difficult for Japanese officials to see why they shouldn't do the same thing.[5]

5. "A No-Fault Deal with Japan," by J.W. Anderson, *The Washington Post* op-ed page, May 26, 1983.

This statement came not from a Japanese spokesman defending his own government, but from an editorial page staff member of a major American newspaper that has given extensive coverage to Japan, including much that is sharply critical. It might also be noted that the first president of MCTC is a retired U.S. naval officer, Bobby R. Inman, who previously had served as Director of the National Security Agency, one of the most sensitive American intelligence organizations, and, in his last governmental position before leaving to join this new firm, as Deputy Director of the Central Intelligence Agency. Surely one can understand how some Japanese might find in all this a rather supportive government-business relationship.

2. Not only can the protectionist argument be turned around in the eyes of many Japanese, but American (and other) critics overlook certain facts when they talk about an imbalance in trade barriers. In a speech delivered in Kansas City in May 1982, this is how Japan's Ambassador to the United States, Yoshio Okawara, put it:

> The once-closed Japanese market is now, in every formal sense, one of the most open and accessible markets of all the advanced industrial countries. Even before the Tokyo Round reductions, Japan's weighted average tariff on dutiable items was 6.9 percent, compared to 8.2 percent for the United States and 9.7 percent for the European Community. After the Tokyo Round reductions are completed, Japan's average tariff on all items will be 3 percent, compared to 4 and 5 percent for the United States and the EC, respectively....Overall, Japan's tariffs are the world's lowest. On most major items in our bilateral trade, Japan's tariffs are comparable to U.S. tariffs.[6]

3. Japanese take frequent (and frequently exasperated) exception to American lamentations about the difficulty of penetrating Japanese markets, pointing to what they consider inadequate efforts on the part of many American companies. The desire of U.S. managers to see a quick return on investment, the unwillingness to devote time and accept the need to develop Japanese language skill, and the lack of understanding of what is going on in Japan by those who sit in headquarters back in the United States—these and other factors are regularly cited as preventing better American performance in Japan's marketplace. At least some U.S. companies that will take the necessary time and effort have turned in highly successful performances—a record that critics of U.S. complaints understandably are quick to mention.

6. "U.S.-Japan Economic Relations," a speech delivered at the Society of American Business and Economic Writers, Kansas City, Missouri, May 4, 1982, published in *Speaking of Japan*, December 1982, Keizai Koho Center, Japan Institute of Social and Economic Affairs, pp. 26-29.

Support for this Japanese position was voiced in the fall of 1983 by an interesting and directly involved observer, Edson W. Spencer, chairman of Honeywell Inc., and chairman of the Advisory Council on Japan - U.S. Economic Relations. While specifically critical of Japan for some of the reasons mentioned in the previous section, Spencer also made the following point:

> Even faced with the tough challenge from Japan, the American electronics industries can compete effectively. A number of American companies have already demonstrated that they can get ahead in the Japanese domestic market. These firms have generally been in Japan a long time, have combined understanding parent-company support with competent Japanese management, and have been patient in waiting for their investments to pay off. A few examples of American electronic companies that have succeeded in Japan for decades are IBM, Texas Instruments, Sperry, Xerox, Burroughs, NCR, and Honeywell. These companies have all participated profitably in the Japanese economy, as effective competitors and responsible public citizens.[7]

4. At least some of the complaints made by the U.S. side also overlook another reality in current economic competition between the two countries. Many American products have lost out to Japanese counterparts because Japanese (and American) buyers prefer the Japanese model. American industry has suffered from a failure to reinvest in new plant, American workers have become too concerned with wage hikes and not enough with the quality of what they put out, and American management has become overly concerned with the drive for short-run profits instead of long-run growth, Japanese and other observers say. The results of these developments—all of U.S. making and all both short-sighted and self-destructive in effect—should not, in Japanese eyes, be pushed off onto Japan. To blame Japan for the failures of the American economy makes little practical sense (although many Japanese acknowledge it does have a logical political value in the United States, just as defending inefficient Japanese agriculture, for example, has political value in Japan).

5. The heavy emphasis on the bilateral trade imbalance also fails to take into account what to many Japanese is the larger picture. Ambassador Okawara, in the talk cited before, made the following point:

> It is also important to keep in mind that merchandise trade is not the complete measure of any nation's international economic performance. This

7. "Japan: Stimulus or Scapegoat?," by Edson W. Spencer, *Foreign Affairs*, Fall, 1983, p. 133.

is especially true of the United States, the world's largest exporter of services, investment capital, technology licenses, and other trade invisibles. In 1981 the United States had a deficit in its global merchandise trade of $27.8 billion. But the U.S. surplus in invisible trade was $34.4 billion, including a $3.3 billion surplus in invisible trade with Japan. As a result, the United States had a global current account surplus of $6.6 billion.

Japan, in contrast, earned a $20 billion surplus in its merchandise trade with the world (in 1981), but had a deficit of $13.7 billion in its trade in the invisibles. Hence, Japan's global current account surplus was trimmed to $4.7 billion.

6. Finally, at least part of the cause of dollar-yen imbalance has been the very large American budgetary deficits and accompanying high interest rates, which have made the dollar unusually attractive in international money markets. From the Japanese viewpoint, American complaints appear to be indulgence in "sour grapes" and "scapegoating," with Japan targeted for blame for a problem grown in the United States. To the extent that the dollar is made unduly strong as a result of American fiscal and monetary policies, then trying to fault Japan for the dollar-yen imbalance, Japanese officials, commentators, and others say, just doesn't make sense.

PATIENCE, A RARE COMMODITY INCREASINGLY IN DEMAND

If all these arguments and counterarguments leave one with the impression that ongoing U.S.-Japanese trade frictions are complicated, readily open to misunderstanding, and with causes interpreted (or misinterpreted) differently by each side—frequently for domestic partisan advantage—then that impression seems fully justified. It also suggests that satisfactory resolution of bilateral differences will be difficult to attain even in partial measure, and will be a long time in the making. Some of our differences are structural—Japan, for example, with sharply limited natural resources, must import a much higher proportion of the goods it needs to fuel its productive capacity than must the United States —and such disparities will not go away soon, if ever.

Over the next few years, then, patience will be at a premium in economic relations between Japan and the United States.

4 ECONOMIC ISSUES
Who Thinks What?

It should be clear by now that the whole field of perceptions, and how Americans and Japanese assess the realities and the causes of differences between them in the economic arena, are subjects that represent uncertain terrain. At times, our two nations and peoples appear like the proverbial ships passing in the night, unseeing and unaware. At others, the lines of communication are open, but with very different messages and signals flowing in either direction. Given the size and importance of the stakes involved, this is an unsatisfactory and potentially dangerous situation. It needs urgent attention and constant improvement.

What, in point of fact, do Japanese and Americans tend to think about many of the economic issues at hand? What is the level of awareness, and how do they look at both current realities and possible future alternatives? Where do they think fault lies in some of the areas of contention?

AWARENESS OF CURRENT BILATERAL ECONOMIC ISSUES

Both Americans and Japanese appear to be reasonably aware of some of the differences that have come to complicate relations between the two countries. Thus, by very large majorities of 77-13 and 60-24 percent, Americans and Japanese respectively indicated their realization in mid-1983 that there was a trade imbalance between the two partners favoring Japan. In the case of the United States, that preponderant opinion was similar in proportion to what had been registered a year before, and had increased from a 70-5 percent balance in 1978, a reflection of the extensive reporting on the balance of payments issue in the U.S. mass media. In Japan, the situation was comparable, with a shift in the ratio from 53-31 percent recorded in 1979.

There is also majority awareness in both countries on another subject— the voluntary limits Japan has accepted in the number of automobiles it ships to the United States. In the United States, however, it was *just* a majority in 1982 (51-44 percent). Not so in Japan, where there is, expectedly, much broader knowledge of the export limitation (71-11 percent in 1982, moving up to 81-16 percent in 1983). As to approval or disapproval of this ceiling, Americans who know about it show themselves to be generally supportive (68-26 percent in favor). Japanese, on the other hand, show a certain resignation possibly tinged with resentment on the issue (17-15 opposed, with a majority of 54 percent saying "it can't be helped").

On the specific issue of American complaints about lack of equal access to Japanese markets, more than six Japanese citizens in ten (61 percent) say that they have heard or read about such charges. On the more general subject of trade frictions between the United States and Japan, opinion is fairly similar in both countries. Thus 50 and 46 percent of Japanese and Americans, respectively, say they have heard or read recently either "a great deal" or "a fair amount" about such frictions. On the other hand, 34 and 49 percent of Japanese and Americans, respectively, say they have heard or read "only a little" or "hardly anything at all" about the ongoing dispute. This translates into a bare majority in Japan in the more aware category, and a slight plurality in the United States in the less aware group. Indeed, almost three Americans in ten (28 percent) fall into the least knowledgeable segment, as compared to only seven percent among the Japanese. The greater Japanese awareness probably stems from the extensive daily attention—frequently highly sensational in presentation—given this subject in the Japanese media, as well as Japan's stronger national focus on the role of exports in sustaining Japan's economic health.

IMPORTANCE OF ECONOMIC TIES

In both the United States and Japan concern about economic relations and frictions in bilateral trade and other dealings undoubtedly plays a key role in setting the tone of public attitudes. Assessing the situation realistically, Americans and Japanese consider these economic ties to be of major importance for both countries, and especially so for Japan: 81 percent of the American people expressed the view in 1982 that the bilateral trade is either "very" or "fairly" important for Japan's prosperity; 83 percent of the Japanese at that time shared this view, with the proportion climbing to 88 percent in the spring of 1983. Somewhat lower numbers of Americans and Japanese are of the opinion that trade with Japan is similarly important for the United States—69 and 67 percent, respectively, in 1982, rising marginally to 71 and 70 percent a year later.

Since Americans and Japanese alike rank the bilateral economic connection as of great importance to both countries, it is understandable that widespread concern is expressed about the possible impact of current trade frictions on relations between the two countries. Thus, Japanese by a lopsided margin of 59-18 percent were either "very" of "fairly" concerned in 1982, as opposed to "not very" or "not at all" concerned, that these frictions "will seriously damage relations between the United States and Japan." Americans at that time split evenly (47-47 percent) on this issue. A year later, the Japanese concern seemed to have eased somewhat, settling to a ratio of 49-31 percent. In the United States, on the other hand, uncertainty had risen (in healthy fashion) to a balance of 56-38 percent.

BLAME FOR ECONOMIC PROBLEMS

It is clear, then that majorities of both Japanese and Americans are aware of the trade imbalance in Japan's favor, and that large numbers are cognizant as well of the ongoing trade frictions between the two countries. In many quarters, the charge is frequently made that American fixation on these targets represents "scapegoating," with Americans quick to point a finger at Japan, or single it out unfairly. Some survey findings tend to raise questions about the degree to which this allegation finds public acceptance.

When asked whether the trade surplus "is mainly due to problems and weaknesses on the U.S. side which hinder American sales to Japan," or whether instead the surplus is "mainly due to policies and practices in Japan which hinder American sales to Japan," Americans in 1982 apportioned the blame about equally—41 percent assigned fault to the United States, and an identical 41 percent looked at Japan as the culprit. Well into the following year, however, the numbers who found fault principally with the U.S. had climbed to 47 percent, while those blaming Japan had dropped to 37 percent. Many other survey research findings also suggest that Americans have become considerably more restrained and modest (as well, at times, frustrated) in their assessment of the role and capabilities of the United States in the world.[1]

This is a finding that deserves special attention. One can argue that it reflects on the part of many Americans an admirable and mature judgement. With all the adverse press and publicity Japan has received in the ongoing discussions of trade and economic problems, it is a bit surprising, perhaps, to find that Americans are not more one-sided in their blame for the cause of these problems. These responses suggest a more balanced and less accusatory point of view among the American public at large than is sometimes evinced by some of their elected or appointed leaders.

Japanese, on the other hand, are significantly more likely to find fault with the U.S.: 55 percent looked first across the Pacific in 1982, while only 25 percent turned their eyes inward, with the proportion shifting only slightly a year later, to 50-23 percent. This, it is important to note, represents a sharp reversal from findings recorded in 1979 when, by a four-to-three margin, those Japanese aware of the trade surplus found fault with Japan. On this subject, Japanese opinion is moving in a direction critical of the United States.

Similarly, Japanese are more prone than Americans to think Japan is being singled out for criticism on trade matters because it is an Asian nation. Among Japanese, 29 percent believe this to be the case, while a comparable 29 percent say that U.S. criticism would be the same for a Western European nation. Among Americans, on the other hand, there is a sizeable rejection of this proposition: only 17 percent agree with the

1. See, for example, Lloyd A. Free and William Watts, "Internationalism Comes of Age—Again," *Public Opinion*, April/May 1980, pp. 46-50.

idea that Japan is being discriminated against because it is Asian, while 62 percent say that our criticisms of a Western European nation would be the same. To be sure, some of the American responses may reflect a socially induced desire to avoid any accusations of racism, and should be read with that possibility in mind.

THE THREAT PERCEPTION AND PROTECTIONISM

One clear effect of the trade imbalance and its extensive coverage in American media is that Americans have established Japan and its imports as far and away the most serious current and potential foreign threat to the jobs of American workers (see Table 4–1).

Table 4–1.

The United States imports large quantities of goods from around the world for sale here. In the case of countries listed, do you think imports from any of them pose a serious threat *now* to the jobs of American workers? Please tell which countries, if any, pose such a serious threat *today.*

And what about *five or ten years* from now? Please tell which countries, if any, will pose a serious threat to the jobs of American workers *then.*

Countries whose Imports Pose "Serious Threat"	"Now"	"Five or Ten Years from Now"
Japan	74 percent	53 percent
Taiwan	35	23
South Korea	12	11
Mexico	11	15
West Germany	10	10
China	9	18
Canada	2	2
Don't know	13	24

Roughly three Americans in four identified imports from Japan as posing a "serious threat now," while more than half said it would still be such a threat five or ten years in the future. Taiwan, Japan's only close challenger in this threat category, was named by less than half as many.

As noted earlier, this concern over the Japanese challenge has led Americans, much more than Japanese, to support the limits on the numbers of Japanese automobiles shipped to the United States. Such a protectionist bent was also recorded in another study, conducted in March 1982 for the Japan Broadcasting Corporation; at that time Americans by a margin of almost two-to-one (59-33 percent) said they would "be in favor of restricting imports from Japan" if such legislation was introduced in the U.S. Congress.

The expansion of such protectionist views is also suggested by the trend in responses over the years concerning certain propositions related to American purchasing habits, as recorded by The Gallup Organization (see Table 4–2).

Table 4–2.

Recently, would you say that you have become less inclined to buy imported products, more inclined, or haven't you given it much thought?

	Less Inclined	More Inclined	Not Much Thought
1972	40%	9%	51%
1973	34	5	60
1977	42	12	45
1980	42	9	48
1982	50	14	35

While the numbers of those who said they were "more inclined" to buy imported products have increased, they remain in the minority. Those "less inclined" to buy goods from abroad reached the one-in-two level, virtually a majority. And the proportion of those who said they hadn't thought much about their inclination to "buy foreign" or not was at its recorded low, down substantially over the 1980-1982 period (see Table 4–3).

Between 1980 and 1982, the numbers of those who said they were basically uninterested in product origin dropped from three in ten to less than one in five, a decline in the "disinterested" of 11 percentage points. At the same time, the numbers of those who disagreed, saying it was "not true" that they didn't pay attention to where a product came from, jumped 10 points.

Table 4–3.

I don't pay much attention to whether the product I buy is American made or imported.

Statement is	1973	1977	1980	1982
Very true	26%	24%	30%	19%
Somewhat true	30	33	29	31
Not true	42	41	38	48

What we seem to have is larger numbers of Americans showing less inclination to buy imported goods, even as they pay more attention to where a product is made. An enhanced sensitivity about the import issue is certainly there.

FACTORS IN ECONOMIC RELATIONS

When we go beyond generalities concerning trade and economic issues to deal with root causes and possible alternatives, we find many expected areas of disagreement between Japanese and Americans—but also some unexpected areas of agreement.

In a major 1982 study, Americans and Japanese were asked to say which country came first to mind when a variety of factors were mentioned that could apply to either or both: in the figures of Table 4-4, the response preferred by Japanese and Americans is emphasized in each case.

As might be expected, given national pride and normal self-respect, more Japanese and Americans choose to *disagree* and pick their own country over the other in a number of instances: product quality, technology, inventiveness, preference for domestic goods, and negotiating flexibility.

Also as might be expected, given voluminous media reporting on the subjects in question, majorities of Americans and Japanese choose to *agree* and pick the United States as the country of highly paid workers, and Japan as the country of diligent workers and export orientation.

Unexpected perhaps but certainly intriguing is that more Japanese and Americans choose to *agree* that Japan is the country of high

Table 4–4.

| | Applies More To: | | | |
| | US | | Japan | |
	Amer. %	Jap. %	Amer. %	Jap. %
1. Has open markets for foreign imports	**75**	**52**	13	13
2. Makes it easy to import manufactured goods	**76**	**43**	13	17
3. Makes it easy to import food and agricultural products	**52**	**36**	33	30
4. Has high tariffs on imports	20	8	**54**	**58**
5. Has highly paid workers	**87**	**60**	5	15
6. Has diligent workers	21	2	**68**	**81**
7. Businesses make strong efforts to sell abroad	25	5	**58**	7
8. Manufactures high quality goods	**48**	5	40	**75**
9. Has superior technology	**51**	10	36	**70**
10. Develops new technologies	**48**	34	39	**45**
11. Consumers prefer domestic products	**43**	25	39	**41**
12. Makes concessions on trade issues	**56**	12	15	**47**

import tariffs, and the United States is the country of open markets, hospitable to imported manufactured and agricultural products.

Thus, on some of those sensitive questions most actively under dispute among policy makers, business and labor leaders, scholars, and other interested parties in both countries, it appears that the Japanese and American people find themselves in agreement more often than not. Also, a number of statements that reflect key U.S. complaints find substantial and unexpected acceptance in Japan.

PERCEPTIONS OF THE TRADE IMBALANCE

The surprising Japanese agreement with at least some areas of American displeasure is corroborated when we compare responses given by Japanese and Americans concerning the principal causes for relatively low sales of American products in Japan compared with Japanese sales in the United States. When asked in 1982 to pick the most important reasons for this discrepancy, Americans and Japanese answered as shown in Table 4–5.

Table 4–5.

	Americans %/rank	Japanese %/rank
1. High tariffs on imports in Japan	19/3	26/1
2. Japanese government rules make it difficult to import American products	20/2	15/2
3. Complicated distribution system in Japan	3/8	7/3
4. Poor quality of American goods	6/5	7/3
5. High wages in the U.S.	31/1	6/5
6. Japanese prefer products made at home	10/4	5/6
7. American inability to meet Japanese consumer tastes	6/5	4/7
8. Inferior American technology	4/7	3/8
9. Weak U.S. selling efforts in Japan	6/5	2/9

Once again, Japanese look primarily to various domestic barriers to explain low American sales in their country—high tariffs and governmental regulatory obstacles heading the list—placing these well above imputed American weaknesses or inefficiencies. Their views are shared in the main by Americans, with the exception being that the latter see their own high wage scales as the most damaging factor.

What about the other side of the coin—reasons for Japanese success in penetrating the American market? Table 4-6 shows responses given in 1982 by Americans and Japanese on that issue.

For Americans, the purported discrepancy in wage scales once again is seen as the factor working most in Japan's favor—a shibboleth that is open to challenge, since in many industries and professions Japanese

Table 4–6.

	Japanese %/rank	Americans %/rank
1. Lower wages in Japan	6/3	35/1
2. U.S. has relatively open market	2/6	16/2
3. Superior quality of Japanese products	53/1	16/2
4. Japanese ability to meet U.S. consumer tastes	4/4	16/2
5. Strong Japanese selling efforts in the U.S.	4/4	10/5
6. More up-to-date technology in Japan	13/2	9/6
7. Dumping and unfair practices by Japanese firms	1/7	4/7

and American wages are moving close to parity. But it is a very comforting rationale for Americans to take, adding to the impression of unfair Japanese advantage and shifting responsibility away from American shoulders.

Americans also note the relatively open U.S. market as benefiting Japanese interests, the obverse of what we found before for American problems in entering the Japanese market. But Americans see as well several factors that are an implicit acknowledgement of Japanese skill and initiative—Japanese product quality, ability to meet U.S. consumer tastes, and selling efforts in this country.

Japanese, on the other hand, are much more focused in their views on what contributes to Japan's success in exporting to the United States. Overwhelmingly, they point to Japanese product quality and then, far behind in second place, Japan's technological prowess. Neither Japanese nor Americans place much emphasis on the theme pressed by a number of U.S. businessmen, labor leaders, and critics of Japan in official circles—the charge of unfair Japanese business practices, as symbolized by the notion of dumping.

Two similar testings of opinion, conducted in Japan in the spring of 1983 by the Shin Joho Center, and later in the year in the United States by The Gallup Organization for Potomac Associates, came up with strikingly comparable results (see Table 4–7). After having confirmed that Japan sells considerably more industrial and consumer goods to the United States than *vice versa,* interviewers asked respondents to say whether each of a list of specific factors was "very important," "fairly important," "not very important," or "not at all important" in bringing about this trade imbalance. Selections are ranked according to those who picked the "very important" category.

Table 4–7.

	Japan	USA
	%/rank	
1. Higher American wages make U.S. products cost more	23/4	60/1
2. Greater Japanese efforts to sell in the U.S. than American efforts in Japan	27/3	44/2
3. More up-to-date technology in Japan	37/2	40/3
4. U.S. has more open market than Japan	17/7	39/4
5. High tariffs on imports in Japan	22/5	39/4
6. Japanese government rules make it difficult to import American products	17/7	36/6
7. Superior quality of Japanese products	59/1	31/7
8. American inability to meet Japanese consumer tastes	13/9	22/8
9. Complicated Japanese distribution system	19/6	16/9

It was noted earlier that Americans, in pointing to reasons for relatively low sales of U.S. products, were more inclined than Japanese to ascribe this to a "buy Japanese" attitude. Furthermore, when they were asked which country came first to mind on the question of consumers preferring domestic products, the number of Japanese who think of Japan over the United States turned out to be considerably larger than Americans who think of the United States over Japan (16-4 percent).

The presence of a "buy Japanese" bias is supported by other survey findings as well. When Japanese were asked about choosing between products of equal price—a Japanese product or one "made in the United States or another Western country"—only five percent said they would usually choose the Western product. Although 45 percent volunteered that their choice would depend on the product itself, another 40 percent acknowledged a preference for the domestic item. The principal reasons given by those who said they normally would buy Japanese were product quality, a sense of safety in making this choice, or simply a straightforward preference for buying the product made in Japan.

Surveys were also made of actual purchasing habits over the preceding 12 months. Three-quarters of the respondents (76 percent) said neither they nor members of their family had bought anything Western in that period. The only purchase in double-digit figures (12 percent) was clothing, accessories, and shoes—an area of consumer interest among young Japanese in particular that is strongly in evidence when one visits shopping bazaars or the major department stores in Tokyo and other urban centers.

Food (including desserts and snack foods) came next, purchased by 6 percent—a figure almost certainly too low by now, with the very rapid growth (principally in Tokyo, to be sure) of business by McDonald's, Baskin-Robbins, and other American fast-food and takeout chains.

Tobacco products, including cigarettes, had been bought by just 2 percent in the testing of opinion, in line with the general market share for American cigarettes of a bit more than 1 one percent. This low figure is a striking reminder of the aggravation caused by this particular item in market access discussions—as exemplified in Ambassador Mansfield's pointed comments cited earlier.

THOUGHTS ABOUT POSSIBLE NEXT STEPS

Noted above are the rather surprising responses among Japanese asked for reasons underlying current frictions between the United States and Japan. Similar Japanese attitudes were found on what Japan should do (if anything) to ameliorate American market access complaints (see Table 4-8).

Even when offered an alternative ("do nothing") that would remove Japanese responsibility, much larger proportions chose instead to say that Japan should eliminate the barriers that have been at the heart of U.S. complaints and pressures. Indeed, the only choice selected by fewer numbers than the "do nothing" option is one that may reflect a "buy Japanese" attitude—"import more U.S. products."

In bringing this section to a close, one comment deserves to be made on the overall nature of Japanese and American attitudes and perceptions on a variety of difficult and controversial economic topics. The sophistication, good judgement, and reasonable degree of equanimity evident in these responses is something that should give those who make and influence policy reassurance. The willingness to see the other side's point of view, and to accept a share of the responsibility, is testimony to the underlying strength of the relationship.

Table 4–8.

	1982 %	1983 %
1. Reduce tariffs on imported goods	46	34
2. Remove non-tariff barriers	30	32
3. Remove quotas on agricultural products	23	15
4. Limit exports of manufactured goods, such as autos, to the U.S.	16	13
5. Do nothing in particular, as market access is about equal in both countries	10	7
6. Import more U.S. products	8	10

5 THE U.S.-JAPAN ALLIANCE

AN OVERVIEW

In considering the astonishing degree of change in relations between Japan and the United States, nothing is more striking than what we see happening in the field of security and defense links. In less than four decades a conquered and demoralized Japan has become the linchpin of American defense planning in the northern Pacific region, and is now actively wooed as a key military power. Indeed, recent administrations in Washington have pressed Japanese leadership to increase its defense contribution, and expand its military capabilities. The turnabout is remarkable, but it is also one that a number of observers think should be kept under constant and careful review.

Memories do persist. Official pressures from the United States on Japan to accelerate its defense expenditures and to extend its security responsibilities to protect sea lanes up to 1,000 miles from the Japanese home islands, for example, elicit shudders of concern and formal statements of unhappiness from powerful Asian leaders. In similar fashion, when Americans are asked to name the negatives that come first to mind when they think about Japan and the Japanese people, it is Pearl Harbor and the history of World War II that top the list.

For many Japanese as well, the idea of a burgeoning defense establishment is not one that is easy to accept. The horrors of the American nuclear bombings of Hiroshima and Nagasaki remain strong. Antiwar and pacifist sentiment is deeply rooted within the Japanese people. Large numbers find it both repugnant and worrisome that their proven economic and industrial prowess may be channeled into the development of a major military capability.

A personal memory comes to mind, drawn from a symposium on the joint U.S.-Japan security relationship held in Tokyo in the autumn of 1980. At a point in the discussion when the focus was on American insistence that Japan take a larger defense role, one influential Japanese participant asked bluntly, indeed almost poignantly, "Don't you Americans remember Pearl Harbor?"

MEMORIES: WHO DID WHAT TO WHOM?

As this very important and extraordinarily sensitive dialogue and debate continues, and as both sides work toward a revised definition of the appropriate security roles for both countries in the region, it is worth reminding ourselves of one important but often forgotten fact: as we think about the history that underlies our relationship, each of us, Americans and Japanese alike, tend to remember what the other side did to us, and not what we did to them.

Americans remember the Pacific theater in World War II primarily in terms of Japanese perfidy in the "sneak attack" on Pearl Harbor, and of our conquest of "the Japs," allies of Hitler's Nazis and Mussolini's Fascists. Japanese, on the other hand, think of Hiroshima and Nagasaki, and the American Occupation—the former a tragedy unique in the annals of warfare, and the latter certainly a mixed blessing.

Both of these sets of memories are highly emotional, charged with the potential for considerable damage to our ties. One can marvel, in fact, that we have come so far so fast, and that those searing events have given way to a revised appreciation of each other's strengths and weaknesses that is, on the whole, much more positive and constructive. Marvel, but also remember that our past recall can be highly selective, and that present tensions could translate into future instability.

A MUTUAL NEED

Interestingly enough, it would appear that average citizens in both countries have something of a visceral understanding of the complexities and uncertainties of the security relationship that some of these considerations suggest. This is not to say that both sides evaluate these bonds in like fashion, or place equal emphasis on the constituent parts. But there is overall recognition that a secure and stable Japan is in America's interest, just as a secure and stable United States benefits Japan. This mutuality of views needs constantly to be supported and, where possible, enhanced.

Let us look at some of the issues involved, and how Americans and Japanese think about them.

JAPAN'S DEFENSE EFFORTS

It may be useful first to set forth some specifics about the extent of Japan's defense contributions. The numbers, while inadequate in the eyes of many observers, are significant.[1] Japan's defense budget of almost $12 billion is the third largest in the world among nonnuclear armed powers, and the eighth largest overall. Its Self-Defense Forces include the following elements: 13 army divisions; 50 destroyer-type vessels, which amounts to more than twice the number in the U.S. Seventh Fleet, carrying responsibilities for the Western Pacific and Indian Oceans; close to the number of antisubmarine vessels as are maintained by the United States in the Eastern and Western Pacific Command, which again includes the Indian Ocean; and some 400 tactical fighter aircraft, more than the U.S. Air Force in Japan, the Republic of Korea, and the Philippines combined.

On the other hand, the readiness of Japanese forces leaves, by common agreement, much to be desired. A great deal of the equipment is outdated, much of it of World War II vintage. Supplies are short. Airfields need improvement, and pilots do not get adequate inflight training time. There is a general lack of the latest electronic equipment, and command and control is inadequate. Early warning and surveillance capacity is weak. Other problems could be added to this list.

1. The following sources have proved particularly useful for this discussion: Richard L. Sneider, *U.S.-Japanese Security Relations,* Occasional Paper of the East Asian Institute, Columbia University, New York, 1982; Japan Defense Agency, *Defense of Japan 1982,* Tokyo, Japan, 1982; testimony by Francis J. West, Jr., before the Subcommittee on Asian and Pacific Affairs, United States House of Representatives, March 1, 1982; and an unpublished research memorandum prepared by Evelyn Colbert for the United Nations Association of the U.S.A. Japanese-American Parallel Studies Program.

The sums spent by Japan on its defense, however, have advanced steadily and sharply over the past decade and more. The increase from 1971 to 1980, for example, was 332 percent: from 1975 to 1980 it was 168 percent. For fiscal 1983, an increase of better than 7 percent over the 1982 budget was approved, in spite of a freeze or even cuts in most other budget categories. Yet these numbers do not look as impressive when placed against the defense expenditures of the United States and other key allies, especially when viewed as percentages of each country's Gross National Product (see Table 5–1).

Table 5–1. Comparison of Defense Expenditures, 1981 ($ in millions).

Country	Defense Expenditures	
	($)	(% of GNP)
United States	171,023	5.5
Great Britain	28,660	5.1
France	26,008	3.9
West Germany	25,000	3.2
Japan	11,497	0.9
Republic of Korea	4,400	5.7
Australia	3,900	3.0

Thus, Japan ranks far behind Great Britain, France, and West Germany in absolute levels of defense spending effort, and trails those countries, Australia, and the Republic of Korea in relative terms.

Japan has unusually large import requirements: 90 percent or more of its needs for wheat, coal, iron ore, crude oil, and cotton—virtually 100 percent for the last three items. In light of Japan's vulnerability, the relatively low level of defense contribution to the assurance of its security and the protection of sea lanes approaching its shores rankles many foreign observers, including some of Japan's closest friends and supporters.

DEFENSE SPENDING: THE AMERICAN VIEW

In trying to assess the American position on what Japan should do to perform its appropriate defense and security role, it is important to recall first what has been going on within the American body politic on the larger issue of defense spending in general. What Americans think about the adequacy of their own defense outlays must, after all, condition their views on what their friends and allies should do.

The mid-1970s witnessed an important shift in the way that the majority of the American people looked at the world around them. During the previous decade—from the mid-1960s on—Americans had gone through a period of growing introversion, with international concerns replaced by domestic ones. Aside from the specific issue of Vietnam, which dominated the foreign policy agenda, worry about such previously dominant international issues as keeping the country out of war, or the threat of communism, for example, gave way to concerns about the U.S. economy, violence and crime in American life, environmental degredation, and the epidemic of drug use.

This inward-looking mood colored attitudes toward defense spending. Throughout the 1960s and early 1970s, one public opinion survey after another recorded a growing belief among Americans that defense expenditures were adequate, if not excessive. Increasing U.S. involvement in Vietnam did not stem rising support for this belief. Rather, as the war continued and chances of battlefield or diplomatic success looked increasingly remote, public backing for more defense spending diminished steadily.

The end of the war in Vietnam and the painful experience of American withdrawal in defeat did not, however, bring with it further diminution in the public's taste for spending on national defense. Public reaction was, in fact, quite the opposite. Frustration, concern about U.S. ability to defend itself adequately, disillusionment with détente, recognition of the need to reinforce key alliance relationships, and uneasiness about a weakened American position globally, among other factors, produced a remarkable consensus in favor of increasing the U.S. defense budget. One study that measured attitudes of Americans between 1974 and 1976 toward federal spending in 23 program areas, both domestic and international, found that in only two fields had there been a net increase in support for greater investment—military and defense spending, and maintaining American military bases abroad.[2]

Speaking broadly, this public backing for defense spending remained consistent until the past year or so. Where there has been any weakening, it has been related either to concern about the state of the economy

---

2. William Watts and Lloyd A. Free, *State of the Nation III*, (Lexington, Mass., Lexington Books, 1978), pp. 60-64 and 161-166.

and potential inflationary damage, or to administration emphasis on the Pentagon budget—both very much a feature of the 1982/1983 budget debate.

Given this generally perceived need for keeping U.S. defense expenditures at least at current levels, it should come as no surprise to find that sentiment among Americans has moved steadily over recent years in favor of Japan's assuming a larger portion of its own security burden. Within the security-related issues on the current U.S.-Japan bilateral agenda, none has drawn more attention in the press and elsewhere, and none has generated more American criticism of Japan's performance, than has this subject. For some time, the focus in Washington was on getting Japan past the "1 percent barrier," to increase its level of defense spending as a proportion of Gross National Product.

A combination of the pressures and realities of Japanese politics with antiwar sentiment in Japan have served to frustrate and curtail significant Japanese action on defense spending—significant, that is, in the eyes of many U.S. policymakers. Even absolute increases in defense expenditures at a time of cutback or holding the line in other budget categories—looked upon by Japanese leaders as a considerable concession to American pressure, undertaken at considerable political risk—consistently have been seen by many Americans as inadequate, as the survey results show (Table 5–2).

Table 5–2.

Under the provisions of the Japanese constitution approved by the American military occupation after World War II, Japan can have only limited military forces for defense. Some Americans believe that Japan should contribute more toward its own defense, and not continue to depend so heavily on the United States. Other Americans feel that a rearmed Japan might become a threat to the security of America or its allies. How do you, yourself, feel about this—do you think Japan should build up a larger military force for defense, or not?

	1978	1980	1982
Should build larger military force	46%	53%	56%
Should not build larger military force	37	36	26
Don't know	17	11	18

Within a span of just four years, support among Americans for Japan's assuming a larger share of its defense burden moved from a slight plurality to a majority of better than two to one. The fact of this majority suggests considerable trust for a former adversary, as well as a desire to see our own defense burdens eased. In this regard, Prime Minister Nakasone's active support for an increased Japanese security role strikes a responsive chord among Americans, even as it stirs wide debate in Japan.

THE "FREE RIDE" AND "LINKAGE" ISSUES

We will turn to a discussion of levels of support for a greater Japanese defense commitment shortly. Two related aspects of that issue, however, deserve attention here.

"Free Ride"

First is the question of the so-called "free ride"—whether Japan spends too little on defense and relies excessively on the United States to maintain security. This subject can have inflammatory impact on public opinion, bringing out strong American feelings on "fairness." It is also a sore point for many Japanese, who feel that the United States does not give sufficient credit to Japan for its role in accepting and supporting—at considerable expense—U.S. forces stationed in and near Japan.

Be that as it may, on the "free ride" issue we have found surprisingly parallel views among Americans and Japanese at large, as the questions and their responses indicate (Table 5–3).

Table 5–3.

Some Americans say that Japan spends too little on defense and relies too much on the United States, in effect getting a "free ride." Do you tend to think this criticism is fair or unfair (asked of Americans)? accurate or inaccurate (asked of Japanese)?

	Americans	Japanese
Fair/accurate	48%	32%
Unfair/inaccurate	35	25
Don't know	17	43

As is frequently the case in public opinion surveys, especially when the focus is on foreign policy matters, a larger proportion of Japanese expresses no opinion than Americans (who generally are ready, it would appear, to give their view on almost any topic). But the proportion of Japanese who accept the "free ride" charge as "accurate" is strikingly close to the American proportion that sees it as "fair."

It would, of course, be insensitive and probably counterproductive to use such results as justification for American policymakers to press the "free ride" theme with excessive vigor on their Japanese counterparts. But the existence of this parallelism in views does suggest that the "free ride" is not so one-sided an opinion as is frequently assumed.

Given the number of clear conflicts that do exist in other areas pertaining to military and security questions, it is almost certainly helpful to be able to identify those areas where differences are minimal— especially if this happens in regard to subjects where the conventional wisdom has it that there *are* strong differences in perceptions.

"Linkage"

Closely related to the "free ride" issue is the question of whether Japan gets a special economic advantage from its relatively low levels of defense spending. If so, should these two aspects of the U.S.-Japan bilateral relationship be linked? Should Japan, in other words, respond to American importunings about doing more in the security area because there is such a massive trade imbalance favoring Japan? Does Japan have a greater responsibility because of the competitive edge it presumably has held over the years?

As we will see shortly, the Japanese people are only marginally in favor of increased defense expenditures, and opposed both to much of a buildup in the Self Defense Forces and to any effort to develop a defense capability apart from the United States. But Japanese do not go one step further, as Americans are moderately more inclined to do, and read into their security dependence on the United Sates a linkage with the economic environment. Thus, when confronted with two contrasting propositions that look at a possible causal link between low defense outlays and economic achievement, Americans and Japanese draw opposite conclusions (Table 5–4).

Table 5–4.

Some people say that Japan has become strong economically because it has spent relatively little on defense.

Others disagree and say that the level of Japan's defense spending has had little or nothing to do with its economic success.

Which view is closer to your own?

	Japanese	Americans
Spending relatively little on defense has helped Japan become strong economically	23%	43%
Level of defense spending has had little or nothing to do with Japan's economic success	38	37
Don't know/no opinion	39	20

Unlike the parallelism in views on the "free ride" issue, the proportions in the two countries on this subject are reversed. A plurality of Americans believe that Japan has benefited economically from its reduced defense expenditures, while a plurality of Japanese thinks just the opposite.

There is also a difference of viewpoint over whether Japan has a responsibility to react favorably to American requests for greater defense spending, in light of Japan's substantial trade surplus (Table 5–5).

Table 5–5.

Some people say that since Japan has a large trade surplus with the United States it should respond positively to American requests to strengthen its own defenses.

Others disagree and say that trade and defense issues are not related and should be kept separate.

Which is closer to your own view?

	Japanese	Americans
Respond positively	7%	42%
Keep two issues separate	61	45
Don't know/no opinion	32	13

On this theme, Americans show a greater degree of ambivalence, with roughly equal proportions accepting each proposition. For Japanese, however, no such uncertainty exists. Among those with an opinion, overwhelming support is registered for the "no linkage" theme.

DEFENSE SPENDING: THE JAPANESE VIEW

Although support for limited but meaningful improvements in Japan's military defense capabilities has been increasing among many in her leadership community, the public as a whole remains cautious in its approach. It is also generally ignorant of the actual levels of current Japanese spending on its security needs. Thus, when asked what they thought was being spent on defense as a proportion of GNP, Japanese responded in mid-1982 as shown in Table 5–6.

Table 5–6.

About 1 percent	29%
1-2 percent	24
About 5 percent	10
About 10 percent	2
Don't know	35

Interpreted narrowly, this means that less than three Japanese in ten are aware that defense spending has been kept under 1 percent. Nearly half are either far wide of the mark or have no opinion. This range of views and absence of accurate information on a subject that has been given such prominence in the Japanese media suggest that leaders in Japan may have more flexibility on defense spending than is often thought—but not an open checkbook.

Japanese regularly evince real pride in the record of burying the militarism of the 1930s. That, combined with strong pacifist sentiment, results in a "don't rock the boat" attitude on altering current defense expenditures. Japanese with an opinion are inclined toward the status quo (Table 5–7).

Table 5–7.

Great increase	4%
Increase a little	21
Keep at present level	30
Reduce	15
Don't know	30

Among those who do favor an increase, reasons given most frequently are: the Soviet threat, defense of Japan needs strengthening, it would give Japan a larger voice in international affairs, and—in last place—it would preserve good relations with the United States.

That pleasing the United States is the least-cited reason suggests that U.S. pressure is not the best way to influence the Japanese public. Indeed, the premier position given the Soviet threat—enhanced, undoubtedly, by the shooting down of a Korean Air Lines passenger plane close to the Japanese border in the late summer of 1983—is a signal that this issue has gained new credibility in Japan, and that the leadership perceptions generally shared in both countries have begun to take a wider hold in Japan.

It is one thing to think in abstract terms about budgetary levels, potential threats, and the like. It is quite another matter, however, to turn to specific operational and policy alternatives. When this was included as part of a major 1982 survey (and partially updated in 1983, with those results—virtually unchanged from the previous year—included in parentheses), considerable ambivalence and uncertainty was found in Japan. Support for some defense-related policy propositions was offset by opposition to others, and in all the areas tested the largest proportion of the public had no opinion (Table 5–8).

On these subjects, pluralities favor an improved warning system, an extension of sea-lanes protection to 1,000 miles, and a blockade of the key straits that would keep Soviet naval forces bottled up in the Sea of Japan. But the largest plurality comes out *against* an increase in the size of the Self Defense Forces, in proportions that correspond fairly closely to sentiments expressed on defense spending.

The absence of much change between views held in 1982 and those registered a year later bears testimony to Japanese conservatism on defense issues. While the public may be more conscious of the Soviet threat, and ready according to some measurements to see limited growth in overall defense spending, it is clear that there is no groundswell for a substantially larger Japanese security role.

Table 5–8.

I'm going to read you some views people have on national defense issues. As I read each one, please tell me whether you tend to agree or disagree.

	Agree	Disagree	Don't know
Japan *needs* to improve its warning system against possible enemy attacks	35%	18%	47%
Japan *does not need* to be able to protect its sea lanes within a 1,000 mile radius	22 (23)	26 (28)	52 (49)
Japan *needs* to be able to blockade the three straits (Soya, Tsushima, Tsugaru) connecting the Sea of Japan with the Pacific in case of emergency	30 (31)	19 (20)	51 (49)
Japan *does not need* to revise domestic laws to permit the Self-Defense Forces to respond quickly in case of military emergency	26	24	50
Japan *needs* to increase the size of the SDF	17 (19)	39 (40)	44 (41)

DIFFERING ASSESSMENTS OF THE SOVIET THREAT

One of the major frustrations for many Americans directly involved with U.S.-Japan security questions has been the apparent reluctance of the Japanese people in general, and much of their leadership, to give credence to American concerns about the the Soviet threat. For a number of observers, the Japanese attitude has seemed to be a refusal to accept an obvious—and increasingly dangerous—reality. Critics of

Japan have seized upon this as another example of what they view as Japan's ability to package issues to Japan's advantage, all the while evading larger responsibilities commensurate with growing power. This sentiment is at the heart of the "free ride" controversy. Why, it is frequently heard, should the United States assume so much of Japan's defense burden, particularly now that Japan has the wherewithal to do so much more?

It is worth exploring for a moment the differing bases for American and Japanese perceptions of the Soviet threat. These differences in perspective can lead to large variations in the policies that ensue.

Ever since the post - World War II relationship between the United States and the Soviet Union began to degenerate into the Cold War, American assessments of the Soviet challenge have been global. The United States sees it as a duty to counter Soviet expansionism at any turn. In doing this, of course, the United States has felt impelled in part by the absence of anyone else able and willing to pick up the charge. Confronting actual or threatened Soviet hostility became central to the foreign policy of one administration in Washington after another.

The Japanese view of the Soviet threat, and what to do (or not do) about it has been much more benign. It is probably fair to say that many Japanese, including (until recently, at least) many leaders, have seen American concern about the Soviet Union and its actions as overstated and even, at times, unduly provocative. Beyond that, Japanese leaders have taken the position that Japan's location—close to the Soviet Union and far removed from its American military protector—forced it into a position where downplaying of confrontation with Moscow was a sensible course to follow.

This is not to suggest that the Soviet Union is any more popular in Japan than it is in the United States. Indeed, in both countries the USSR is regularly recorded in opinion surveys as one of the least admired nations on earth. It is also viewed just as regularly as the principal threat to peace. But those parallel perceptions do not translate automatically into parallel definitions of policy.

The accession to the Prime Minister's office of Yasuhiro Nakasone in late 1982 brought to the forefront for the first time a national leader prepared to deal far more directly with the Soviet threat. But it is worth recalling that his characterization during an early visit to Washington of Japan's role in its alliance with the United States as that of a "big aircraft carrier" (improperly translated at first as "unsinkable") caused an eruption of protest in Japan, sent his popularity ratings into a tailspin, and caused him quickly to moderate his public comments. In addition, the initial Soviet response, to confirm targeting of Japan with Soviet SS-20 missiles in Soviet Asia, both angered the Japanese even as it confirmed many in their view that confrontation was not the best way to do business with Moscow.

The steady buildup of Soviet forces in Asia has, however, moved Japan toward greater willingness to do more on the military/security front. The presence of the SS-20s, the major increase in Soviet naval strength in the Pacific (which now comprises about two-fifths of the total Soviet fleet), including the Minsk carrier force, a greatly augmented submarine fleet, and access to the excellent harbor facilities at Cam Ranh Bay in Vietnam, and regular "Backfire" and other aircraft activities in the area, all have served to command the greater attention of Japanese leaders. Also, the public was stunned by the Soviet destruction of an unarmed Korean Air Lines plane in the late summer of 1983.

One result of this revised Japanese perspective has been a subtle shift in the framework of security discussions between American and Japanese officials. The emphasis on breaking the "1 percent barrier," mentioned above, has been replaced in some of the working forums by a stress on "roles and missions." That new thrust has been directed at trying to reach agreement on what is expected of each party in the alliance, rather than getting bogged down in arguments about specific budgetary levels.

Whether this modified approach can lead to improvement in Japanese defense capabilities remains to be seen. Such an enhancement has drawn increasing support from experts and specialists in both countries,[3] even as they try not to incite fears of a new wave of militarism sweeping the country, in a replay of the 1930s.

THE MUTUAL SECURITY RELATIONSHIP: BENEFITS, RESPONSIBILITIES, AND EVALUATION

In all the discussion and at times heated rhetoric concerning the U.S.-Japan security relationship, one fundamental point seems either lost or overlooked: to a remarkable degree, this relationship is taken for

---

3. See, for example, *The Japanese - American Alliance: A Framework for the Future*, a Joint Report by the United Nations Association of the USA and the Asia Pacific Association of Japan (New York: UNA/USA, 1983).

granted by both sides. The U.S.-Japan alliance is seen—especially by responsible leaders in both countries—as essential to well-being and security, both individual and joint.

To put the proposition more dramatically, just think what the security picture in northeast Asia would look like if Japan and the United States abandoned their alliance. And not only there: the implications for global stability are staggering. The two countries need each other. It surely behooves all who bear responsibility for this relationship, whether official or unofficial, to keep this reality in mind. To support actions or policies that would have the effect of driving the two countries apart would represent a tragic short-sightedness that future generations could neither tolerate nor understand.

A New Acceptance

This is a far cry from the situation that prevailed not long ago. Recall the riots that swept Tokyo in 1960, when President Eisenhower was on his way to participate in ceremonies linked to the signing of the Treaty of Mutual Cooperation and Security. At one point, the official car carrying Ambassador Douglas MacArthur III and Presidential Press Secretary James Haggerty was stormed and the occupants terrorized by the rampaging crowds. Eisenhower himself was forced to cancel his visit to Japan and proceed directly on to Korea, in dramatic confirmation of just how dangerous the situation in Japan was.

By now, however, that same treaty is accepted, with only limited pockets of opposition. Furthermore, with the consolidation of U.S. forces in Japan onto fewer bases and the reversion of Okinawa to Japanese rule in 1971, the American military presence is no longer the thorny issue it once was. In fact, the 1982 proposal by the U.S. Department of Defense to station F-16 fighter aircraft at an airbase at Misawa was greeted in Japan with equanimity. Even a subject as sensitive as nuclear weapons transiting Japanese ports aboard U.S. naval vessels, broached in a May 1981 interview by former Ambassador Edwin O. Reischauer, faded rather rapidly after the uproar that his remarks initially—and predictably—caused.

Who Benefits?

If there is general acceptance of the treaty/security relationship, however, there is also disagreement as to who is its principal beneficiary. When asked, Japanese and Americans revealed very different views on this subject (Table 5–9).

Table 5–9.

	Americans		Japanese	
	1982	*1983*	*1982*	*1983*
More beneficial to Japan	40%	36%	19%	13%
More beneficial to the U.S.	6	6	21	31
Benefits both about equally	40	39	26	26
Don't know	14	19	34	30

When those who rate the treaty as mutually beneficial are removed from the picture, the remainder divide quite differently: Americans predominantly see Japan as getting the most out of the relationship, while Japanese split more evenly between those who think Japan comes out ahead and those who think the United States does. But there has been a shift in Japanese opinion over the past year: those who believe the United States gains the most have increased substantially in number, even as the number of those who think Japan is the principal beneficiary has dwindled.

It may be natural that among those who see one country deriving special benefit, it is the *other* country that gains. There is, however, some cause for concern. To the extent that the "free ride" and "linkage" issues remain a staple of the security discussion, those people who think it is the other side that comes out ahead can become increasingly irritated over what they perceive to be an inequitable balance in the relationship. That irritation, of course, can spill over into other areas.

Japan's Roles

In considering certain aspects of the security relationship, and the role Japan should or might play, Japanese again show the ambivalence we noted earlier when discussing Japanese views on defense spending (Table 5–10; relevant updated 1983 findings are shown in parantheses).

Table 5–10.

	Agree	Disagree	Don't know
Japan *should* pay a larger share of the costs of stationing U.S. forces in Japan	7% (6)	48% (50)	45% (44)
Japan *should not* conduct joint maneuvers with U.S. forces	34	23	43
Japan *should* share its defense related technology with the U.S.	25 (24)	27 (29)	48 (47)
Japan *should not* develop a defense capability independent of the U.S.	38 (36)	15 (15)	47 (49)

Among those with an opinion, responses to the first three propositions—and especially the first two—indicate a reluctance that Japan should assume a greater role in bilateral security. Yet the "go-it-alone" philosophy is rejected by a margin of better than two-to-one. The Japanese public shows little inclination to favor any major shifts in current security arrangements—a position that has changed almost not at all over the past year, in spite of (or perhaps because of?) Prime Minister Nakasone's outspoken emphasis on the need for Japan to take a more active security posture. Recall that the decision announced by the prime minister just before his January 1983 visit to Washington to proceed with sharing of defense-related technology added fuel to the controversy surrounding that trip. As our figures suggest, such sharing of technology does not command widespread public support, being opposed by a small (and unchanged) plurality.

It is also worth noting the extent to which Japan helps pay the costs of stationing U.S. troops in Japan (a share, as we have just seen, that concerned Japanese do not wish increased). According to Assistant Secretary of Defense Francis J. West, Japanese expenditures in 1981 came to $21,000 for each of the 46,000 servicemen in Japan; the comparable cost sharing for the 245,689 troops in West Germany was $5,400.[4] On a per capita basis, Japan's contribution is about four times that of West Germany's.

The Japanese View: Deterrence, not Defense?

If we look at a number of the indicators of public sentiment reported thus far, we are struck by what appears to be a paradox. The Japanese people, on the whole, are cautious in their assessments of Japan's security role. Increased defense spending is viewed with moderate approval. An enhanced security capability—in the form of a larger SDF, expanded defense assignments either within the home islands or in the adjoining region, or closer involvement with the U.S. military establishment—is not accepted with much fervor. Indeed, surveys commissioned over the years by the Japanese Prime Minister's Office have recorded many Japanese as preferring either unarmed resistance or no resistance at all in the event Japan were attacked.

Alongside this pacifism, however, is substantial opposition to Japan's developing a defense capability independent of the United States: the ratio against this proposition is five-to-two among those with an opinion, certainly indicating little backing for a unilateral security effort.

But the contradiction here may be more apparent than real. What the Japanese people may be saying, in a very self-interested and logical manner, is that the current situation is not all that bad. Japan remains under the American security umbrella, and should do about what it is doing, or perhaps a bit more, but that is enough. As long as the American security commitment holds up (which, as we shall see shortly, is something many Japanese are unsure about), why expand Japanese capabilities, and thereby possibly expose Japan more directly to external (read Soviet) threat? Why, in other words, "rock the boat?"[5]

4. Testimony before the House Subcommittee on Asian and Pacific Affairs, March 1, 1982.

5. American attitudes toward the security of South Korea reflect a similar ambiguity better called self-interest. Even when former President Jimmy Carter pressed the idea of withdrawing U.S. ground troops from Korea, the American public remained consistently opposed, as they have been both before and since. Yet Americans also express, by slight pluralities, opposition to defending South Korea should North Korea attack again. Americans evidently do not favor the idea of another land war in Asia, especially on behalf of a nation they view negatively on a number of points; but they also do not wish to see U.S. troops pulled out, since, presumably, they have helped to maintain stability on the peninsula. Again, "why rock the boat?" See Richard L. Sneider and William Watts, *The United States and Korea: New Directions for the '80s* (Washington, D.C. Potomac Associates, 1980).

What this suggests is a tendency to think more in terms of deterrence than defense, a line of reasoning that naturally could hold much appeal for Japanese who see themselves as isolated and threatened. That it may also mean a loss of Japan's sovereignty to the American protector could become increasingly unacceptable over time. This may be especially true for a new Japanese generation with no direct links to the experience of World War II and the postwar relationship between the two countries.

SECURITY COMMITMENTS: HOW STRONG?

In the final analysis, a key feature of the relationship between friendly nations is the willingness of each one to go to the defense of the other if attacked by a common enemy. The U.S.-Japan link is remarkable in this regard, since the commitment goes in one direction only: the joint security guarantee is for the protection of Japan, not the United States. In spite of the various and growing aggravations that have become a staple of current ties between the two countries, the continued willingness of Americans to support the defense of Japan is, like the security link itself, remarkable.

Trends in Levels of Support

Let us look, for example, at the comparative willingness of Americans over the past decade and more to defend Japan and key allies in Western Europe (Table 5-11).

Table 5-11.

Please tell me whether you agree or disagree with the following statements:
1. The United States should come to the defense of its major European allies with military force if any of them are attacked by Soviet Russia.
2. The United States should come to the defense of Japan with military force if it is attacked by Soviet Russia or Communist China.

	1972	1974	1976	1978	1980	1982	1983
1. Europe							
Agree	52%	48%	56%	62%	74%	64%	65%
Disagree	32	34	27	26	19	25	25
Don't know	16	18	17	12	7	11	10
2. Japan							
Agree	43%	37%	45%	50%	68%	54%	57%
Disagree	40	42	37	35	28	30	29
Don't know	17	21	18	15	4	16	14

1974: Beginnings of Strengthened Internationalism

In retrospect, it appears that 1974 was an important turning point for Americans in their willingness to commit U.S. military might to assist either our key European allies or Japan. That year, as the war in Vietnam was moving to its tragic and humiliating end, Americans seem to have concluded that this was not the time to turn their backs on major friends. Rather, as these figures clearly indicate, they started moving in the opposite direction—toward supporting the security of countries accepted as important to the United States.

That trend continued at least until 1980, and was accompanied throughout the latter half of the 1970s by a steady increase in public backing for more defense spending and a refurbishing of U.S. military capabilities. Contrary to much popular wisdom, the immediate effect of defeat in Vietnam was *not* a resurgent isolationism among the American people. Instead, they took a look around, were disturbed by a more hostile and less tractable international environment, and came to a logical conclusion—shore up security relationships with those partners seen as key to U.S. national interests, and make sure as well that U.S. defenses are what they should be.

Japan, as the survey results show, fits the picture. While the support levels for defense of Japan do not match those for Europe, they don't lag all that far behind. When we examine the views of various leadership groups in the United States, Japan's security regularly has ranked very near the top of the scale, almost on a par with Europe's.[6]

Indeed, the level of commitment actually *rose* (albeit marginally) from 1982 to 1983, after a very substantial dropoff from the high point of 1980. Whether this is another indicator of greater realism in American understanding of the importance of the relationship—as we speculated in Chapter 2—remains to be seen. It is, in any event, encouraging.

Post-1980: Looking a Bit More Inward?

If 1974 marked the start of increasing support for military defense of Japan and nations in Europe, 1980 seems to have been the year when such support peaked. And just as Americans showed strong approval of expanded U.S. defense budgets during the second half of the 1970s, so also did that approval dwindle as the next decade unfolded.

The causes for this moderately more introspective public mood undoubtedly are multiple. Certainly the ailing American economy had a lot to do with it, as Americans found high inflation rates, high levels of unemployment, high interest rates, and a soaring cost of living all conspiring to focus their attention inward. Faced with massive budget deficits, the full implications of which may not have been understood, Americans looked at the gargantuan defense bill as a logical place to start cutting—or at least limiting. Far better to do some chopping there, for example, than to sacrifice a variety of social programs or entitle-ments that had come to be taken for granted.

Another factor that came into play was the spreading concern that programmed weapons increases had surpassed legitimate requirements, and were instead producing a new danger. The nuclear freeze movement in the United States, which found resonance in Western Europe, was testimony to this sentiment. And, one can argue, some of the Reagan Administration rhetoric did little to calm people's jangled nerves. Many came to the conclusion that some top officials went too far in some of their pronouncements. The public reaction, under the circumstances, was to call for greater restraint, greater attention to arms control, and a curb on increases in defense outlays.

Finally, one can argue that 1980 was a year when Americans felt a

6. See, for example, William Watts, *The United States and Asia: Changing Attitudes and Policies*, (Lexington, Mass: D.C. Heath and Co., 1982), and *American Public Opinion and U.S. Foreign Policy 1983*, Chicago: Chicago Council on Foreign Relations, 1983.

particular sense of urgency about alliances faced with the twin crises of the Iranian hostage seizure and the Soviet invasion of Afghanistan. While other traumatic events have surfaced since, these two did, at the time, focus American opinion in dramatic fashion.

JAPANESE SKEPTICISM

It is worth noting again the very substantial numbers of Americans who remain committed to protecting Japan's security and territorial integrity even during a period when bilateral relations are strained. By the late summer of 1983, shortly after former Ambassador Ushiba expressed dismay at the tone of comments about Japan he encountered on a return trip to Washington, the American people by a margin of close to two-to-one stated their willingness to defend Japan with U.S. military forces. And, as noted above, this margin had actually improved over the previous year.

The overall ebbing since 1980—now perhaps stabilized—must not, however, be ignored. It leaves many Japanese apprehensive. Their sense of the reliability of the U.S. security assurance appears much less certain than Americans themselves express. Indeed, it seems to have diminished a bit in recent years, as responses to a question asked in Japan indicate (Table 5–12).

If the first two groups with an opinion are grouped together as being on the positive side, and the second two clustered on the negative, the positive-negative balance moves in the pattern shown in Table 5–13.

What had been in 1981 a plurality expressing at least a "fair amount" of confidence in the United States to come to Japan's defense turned into a considerably larger plurality just two years later for "not very much" faith in the American commitment. That pessimism, which many would say is part of the Japanese character, still does not suggest popular trust in Japan in the relationship.

Table 5–12.

In the event our country's security were threatened by a Soviet attack, how much confidence do you feel we could have in the United States coming to our defense—a great deal, a fair amount, not very much, or none at all?

	1981	1982	1983
Great deal	3%	11%	9%
Fair amount	37	24	22
Not very much	34	34	39
None at all	3	6	7
Don't know	23	25	23

Table 5–13.

	Positive	Negative
1981	40%	37%
1982	35	40
1983	31	46

A Cautionary Note

As one reflects on some of the observations set forth in the preceding pages, there is much room for encouragement in the way the U.S.-Japan security relationship has broadened and matured in recent years. There is also proper place for satisfaction over the way that the peoples of both countries have come to accept this revised framework, even if some real pockets of skepticism remain.

But it would be foolish not to recognize that there are areas for concern. Not only have official exchanges on security matters often been carping and tendentious, but certain aspects of the public assessment are worrisome as well. Differing American and Japanese views on Japan's appropriate defense role, on the flow of benefits from the Mutual Security Treaty, on the proper degree of linkage between defense and economic questions, and on burdensharing in general, assuredly (and properly) command a place on the bilateral agenda.

These subjects also represent areas of actual or potential discord that need to be acknowledged and addressed by Japanese and American negotiators and their leaders with greater awareness of the political imperatives and national sensitivities. Such awareness has frequently been lacking in the past, to the very real detriment of all concerned.

6 THE AGE FACTOR
More Problems Ahead?

As we examine the rich tapestry of Japanese and American views, attitudes, perceptions, misunderstanding, and awareness, it is hard not to be impressed by the complexities and subtleties that emerge on both sides. The mosaic, furthermore, is never static, nor are opinions held in the same fashion across the board by different segments of the population in each country.

We find, for example, that those with a college background tend to support those propositions that would strengthen the relationship between the two countries. In each country they place higher value than does the national average on the links that have been forged. And they are more concerned about the effects on our bilateral ties of the ongoing frictions and disputes in the trade and economic areas.

These deviations from the norm are, it should be added, in keeping with survey research in general. The college educated, as well as the more affluent and those in the professional/business/management category, are more likely to hold views that could be called more international or multilateral. They are less inclined to favor isolationist, unilateralist, or protectionist alternatives.

AGE: AN IMPORTANT VARIABLE

Any assessment of national opinion needs to try to answer, "What next?" Do readings of the public mood give any indication of what the future may hold?

In one sense, to be sure, the response must be no. Testings of opinion cannot be held as truly predictive. Events to come, the nature of national leadership, the changing international environment—these and many other factors surely will have their impact on the framework of public opinion as time passes.

In another sense, however, it is useful to look at how people in different age groups respond to a variety of propositions and alternatives. If there are substantial variations according to age in how key national issues are assessed, then those differences may come to have influence on policies and events. Sometimes the results can be dramatic, as occurred in the United States in the late 1960s and early 1970s. Then, the clash in generational perceptions of American policy in Southeast Asia resulted in widespread domestic civil disorder and some loss of life.

EFFECT OF AGE ON OPINION IN AMERICA

Interestingly enough, on many of the issues probed in a major study in the United States, age differences were of marginal importance. To be sure, when Americans were asked to name the most prominent negative thoughts in their minds about Japan, those 50 and older picked Pearl Harbor and World War II in far higher proportions than did those in their mid-30s or younger.

But on the question of support for Japan building a larger military force—one area, for example, where sharp differences in opinion on the basis of age might well be expected—the responses were surprisingly uniform, the variations statistically insignificant (Table 6–1).

Table 6–1.

Age	18-24	25-34	35-49	50+	Average
Japan should build larger military force	54%	56%	57%	56%	56%
Should not build larger military force	29	27	26	25	26
Don't know	17	17	17	19	18

This lack of differentiation, even among those whose memories directly include World War II, is a bit surprising. One can speculate that a limited Japanese defense buildup has become acceptable in roughly equal terms among all age groups simply because Americans are increasingly frustrated at having to bear so much of the security burden themselves.

One set of questions did provoke meaningful differences in views according to age (see Table 6–2). In various character traits, Americans who had passed the half century mark tended to take a distinctly less favorable view of Japanese than did the younger, especially those in the 18 - 24 and 25 - 34 age groups.

Table 6–2.

Age	18-24	25-34	35-49	50+	Average
Creative	71%	68%	67%	64%	67
Imitative	20	27	23	23	23
Don't know	9	5	10	13	10
Peaceful	67	70	65	56	63
Warlike	20	22	23	27	24
Don't know	13	8	12	17	13
Humble	60	64	56	45	54
Arrogant	25	26	26	34	29
Don't know	15	10	18	21	17
Loyal	68	71	65	47	60
Treacherous	17	17	18	32	23
Don't know	15	12	17	21	17
Straightforward	55	63	61	41	53
Deceitful	28	23	23	37	29
Don't know	17	14	16	22	18

Americans 50 and older are somewhat more inclined to think of Japanese as "warlike" than are those younger, and markedly more prone to apply the terms "arrogant," "treacherous," and "deceitful." The World War II memories, which emerged most forcefully among the older group as noted above, find expression in these larger clusterings around the negative alternative.

EFFECT OF AGE ON OPINION IN JAPAN

Among Japanese, the impact of age on opinion appears to be sharper than among Americans, especially on views of defense and security issues now on the bargaining table. Not only is it sharper, but in many instances it is the younger Japanese who are more likely than their elders to be critical of the United States.

Table 6–3 is a tabulation of responses recorded in 1982 and 1983 (where available), broken down by age category, to a number of questions where this age factor appears reasonably strong. Younger and older age groups have been used, and those without an opinion have been omitted. The degree of the importance of age fluctuates, but the message is there nonetheless. (As in the case of the discussion above concerning American responses, the overall import of these questions has been addressed in other chapters.)

Table 6–3.

Age	18-34	50+	18-34	50+
	1982		1983	
1. Preference for Japanese or Western Product				
Japanese	29%	47%	n/a	n/a
Western	6	3	n/a	n/a
It depends	59	39	n/a	n/a
2. Current State of U.S.-Japan Relations				
Excellent/good	21%	27%	16%	25%
Only fair/poor	63	47	61	50
3. Level of Defense Spending				
Increase	21%	29%	n/a	n/a
Keep at present level or reduce	50	36	n/a	n/a
4. Who Benefits More from U.S.-Japan Security Treaty?				
Japan	18%	21%	12%	12%
United States	27	13	37	24
Both about equally	24	26	29	26
5. Confidence in U.S. to Come to Japan's Defense				
Great deal/fair amount	30%	35%	26%	35%
Not very much/none at all	47	34	52	37

Table 6–3. (Con't.)

Age	18-34	50+	18-34	50+
		1982		1983
6. Japan Needs to Improve Its Warning System Against Possible Enemy Attack				
Agree	33%	36%	n/a	n/a
Disagree	22	11	n/a	n/a
7. Japan Needs to Be Able to Blockade the Three Straits				
Agree	29%	34%	26%	37%
Disagree	23	11	24	14
8. Japan Does Not Need to Revise Domestic Laws to Permit the Self Defense Forces (SDF) to Move Quickly				
Agree	31%	18%	n/a	n/a
Disagree	22	27	n/a	n/a
9. Japan Needs to Increase the Size of the SDF				
Agree	14%	23%	14%	26%
Disagree	47	28	46	28
10. Japan Should Pay a Larger Share of Costs for U.S. Forces				
Agree	4%	9%	3%	8%
Disagree	57	40	53	44
11. Japan Should Share Its Defense Technology with the U.S.				
Agree	23%	30%	18%	30%
Disagree	31	19	34	22

As one goes down the list, it is clear that younger Japanese part ways with their elders in a number of important arenas.

The younger Japanese, as compared to their elders, are:

—less inclined to opt for the Japanese product when they do comparison shopping, and tend to take other factors into mind (a fact readily apparent to visitors to Japan from the clothing styles and eating habits of many younger Japanese);

—less positive about the current state of U.S.-Japan relations;

—less in favor of increased defense spending, and more supportive of keeping the budget at current or reduced levels;

—more inclined to think that the United States, not Japan, is the principal beneficiary of the U.S.-Japan Mutual Security Treaty;

—much less confident of the American security commitment to Japan;

—less in favor of taking steps to upgrade Japan's warning system against possible attack;

—less in favor of ensuring the capability of blockading the three straits that control Soviet egress from its Siberian naval bases to the Pacific Ocean;

—much more opposed to changes in Japanese law that would permit the Self Defense Forces to respond more quickly in time of emergency;

—much less supportive of an increase in the size of those Self Defense Forces;

—even more opposed to raising the Japanese contribution for the costs of stationing U.S. troops in Japan, and;

—substantially less willing to share Japanese defense technology with the United States.

The above is a reasonably imposing array of differences. It indicates some fundamental differences in view between younger and elder Japanese, on issues that are themselves fundamental. At a minimum, these differences bear careful watching and further exploration. One can speculate that the seeds of an emergent anti-Americanism, or at least of growing skepticism about the value of ties with the United States, is there.

At this point, the comments made by the young Japanese guest at my friend's home take on additional significance. If, as he said, many of his contemporaries share his sense of "feeling sorry for you (Americans)," and if they also hold the views just noted that are less supportive than their elders' on certain key issues in the U.S.-Japan relationship, then there is plenty of room for concern.

How will younger Japanese perform as they move into positions of greater public and private responsibility? Will their views moderate and become more accepting of the links between the United States and Japan? Or will they want to move Japan in directions less close, less fully tied to the American connection?

It is true that people tend to become more conservative as they grow older. But in this context, what does "conservative" mean? It could—and, hopefully, will—mean a fuller recognition over time by younger Japanese of the importance of the U.S.-Japan relationship. But it could also take a different turn, looking inward and breeding nationalism. To the extent that American policy appears to Japanese to be overly critical, self-serving, and protectionist, the latter alternative may become increasingly attractive.

7 TROUBLES IN THE PARTNERSHIP

Given both the complexity and the intensity of the U.S.-Japan relationship, and the extent to which it has expanded in such a remarkably short period of time, we could expect that communications and mutual understanding between the two sides would steadily improve.

But has that proved to be the case? If the issues that aggravate relations between Japan and the United States are, in turn, serious substantively and dangerous politically, do Americans and Japanese recognize this discord and its meaning? Do both, dedicated enemies once and edgy partners now, give full weight to the importance of that relationship? Do they care about it enough to acknowledge the need for compromise that must support any lasting tie?

A NEW NATIONAL EMPHASIS

One of the uncertainties involved here is the relative suddenness with which current Japan-U.S. discord has surfaced as a U.S. national issue. What had been for many years a subject area reserved for experts and career officials has become daily fare for the American people at large. That is, in many ways, a welcome development. It comes as an antidote to a long period of neglect, and of most Americans taking the U.S.-Japan relationship for granted. Japan, for its part, has never treated these ties so cavalierly; the American link has dominated Japan's international environment in the entire post-World War II era.

Many recent signals provide room for encouragement. Not the least of them is the fact that so many people on *both* sides of the Pacific are now working hard at trying to ease the persistent frictions causing such anguish and, in some quarters at least, anger. Formation of the new U.S.-Japan Advisory Commission, announced by the Japanese and American governments in May 1983, was a helpful step. It was charged with moving beyond the earlier "Wisemen's Group" to seek a better understanding and possible resolution of all areas of discord. The seniority of its membership and the talented support staff provided in both Tokyo and Washington are reassuring signs of the seriousness of this effort.[1] Optimists see promise of thoughtful and innovative recommendations to come.

Furthermore, increased top-level urging toward improved relations has been seen. George P. Shultz, President Reagan's secretary of state and a man with exceptionally strong credentials in international business, finance, and economics, has shown a strong awareness of the stakes involved. Early in his tenure he gave new impetus to improving both the atmospherics and the substance of the relationship. Yasuhiro Nakasone, upon becoming Japan's Prime Minister in late 1982, moved even more vigorously along similar lines. Such nudges and more from top governmental levels in both countries augur well for the future.

If trends in public opinion can be assessed as a useful indicator, such moves—illustrative of the myriad activities being pushed on many

1. The members on the Japanese side are: Nobuhiko Ushiba, former Minister of External Economic Relations and Ambassador to the United States, chairman; Saburo Okita, former Minister of Foreign Affairs and president of the newlyfounded International University of Japan; Akio Morita, chairman of Sony Corporation; Isamu Yamashita, chairman of Mitsui Engineering and Shipbuilding; Yotaro Kobayashi, president of Fuji-Xerox Corporation; Seisaburo Sato, professor at Tokyo University; and Ichiro Shioji, president of the Japan Federation of Autoworkers. Staff support has been entrusted to Tadashi Yamamoto, Director of the Japan Center for International Exchange and an expert on U.S.-Japan relationships. American members include: David Packard, chairman of the board of Hewlett-Packard, Inc., and former Deputy Secretary of Defense, chairman; Donald Rumsfeld, president of G.D. Searle and Company and former Secretary of Defense; James Hodgson, former Ambassador to Japan; Douglas Fraser, former president of the United Automobile Workers of America; Daryl Arnold, chairman of the Western Growers Association; James Bere, chairman of the Borg-Warner Corporation; and William Timmons, former official in the Nixon administration and president of Timmons and Company. Albert Seligmann, Director of the Office of Japanese Affairs in the Department of State at the time of his appointment and one of the U.S. government's key Japan language officers and specialists, has been appointed American staff director.

fronts—came at a moment when they were badly needed. As already discussed in greater detail in Chapter 2, American attitudes overall began to erode from the high levels of 1980, as the Japanese presence became a source not only of interest, admiration, and emulation, but also of concern and threat. This slippage in the United States found a reflection in Japan as well, where constant U.S. pressures on economic and security issues have come to grate more noticeably on Japanese sensitivities.

PROBLEMS THAT PERSIST: A CATALOGUE OF ILLS

The discussion thus far has meant to suggest that the base on which relations between Japan and the United States rests is sound, even though the relations are troubled. Disagreements abound and mutual confidence is being subjected to great strain.

From what seeds do these disagreements and strains spring? Is it possible to isolate a number of elements in the way Japan and the United States do (or don't) do business with each other, or in the makeup of their individual approaches to reality, that may help people in both countries understand the unsatisfactory and potentially destructive framework in which they now find themselves?

The following list of problem areas is not intended to appear unduly negative or pessimistic. Indeed, as discussed in the previous section, there are a variety of factors at work that provide considerable room for optimism. But the fact remains that the United States and Japan are mired in a bad patch. Looking at some of the background causes (and no claim is made that this rundown is exhaustive) may help clear the air and suggest alternative and ameliorative approaches.

Differing Focus

It is surely fair to say that the starting point for at least some American and Japanese perspectives is strikingly different. When looking at various areas of disagreement, particularly economic, each side tends to come from a direction that strengthens its own case and downplays the other side's. Thus, Japanese debate and analysis regularly emphasize broad economic factors as the root causes of the problems in the bilateral relationship. That focus is inherent in much of the Japanese complaint list that we discussed in Chapter 3. On the American side, however, much greater attention is paid to more specific issues—market access, nontariff barriers, industrial targeting, and the like.

By dwelling on broader economic factors and by emphasizing global trading patterns, high U.S. interest rates, comparative economic dynamism, and so forth, Japanese representatives play to their own hand. These are problems and concerns that support the Japanese position. In similar fashion, when American negotiators raise questions about market access, specific tariff or surcharge complaints, and the like, they put the spotlight on topics that lend weight to the American case.

Taking such positions is, from each side's standpoint, only appropriate. But it is also true that this differing focus contributes as well to a perception of unfairness, and the sense that the other party is loading up the argument in his favor, all the while evading the real issues.

The "Misunderstanding Syndrome"

Closely related to differing foci is a subtle but highly pervasive fallacy that by now has become something of a staple in the Japanese-American dialogue—the "misunderstanding syndrome." Thus, over the years it has become very popular in both the United States and Japan—more so in Japan, I believe, with its highly developed sense of separateness—to reason along the following lines: "If only you understood us, then we could work things out satisfactorily." Each protests the best of will, and rationalizes whatever difficulty is currently at hand as primarily a problem of "misunderstanding" by the other side.

There is, however, a fatal flaw in this argument. More often than not, what each side is *really* saying is something closer to this: "If only you understood us, *then you would agree with us.* Then we could work things out satisfactorily, *along the lines that we want.*"

This is an illusion. There is, of course, no way that the United States or Japan can have it all its own way on the very real issues now dividing them. Yet each side persists, in varying degrees, to think that it can. The result is a standoff, accompanied by charges of bad faith and unreasonable obstinacy. Impatience and irritation grow. Protectionist sentiment rises in the United States. Japan feels threatened and increasingly resentful.

Levels of compromise and accommodation are a necessity. Talking benignly about "misunderstanding" only confuses the debate. In a variety of arenas, as evidenced by the conflicting positions described earlier, it is not misunderstanding that is involved. Fundamentally divergent definitions of economic interest or national security can be at stake.

The issue of security links between our two countries is a good case in point. The substantially differing assessments of the Soviet threat and its implications for Japan, as discussed in Chapter 5, have led to widely contrasting policy conclusions (although these may be undergoing some revision now).

It is the same in the economic arena. Once again, "misunderstanding" can in fact mask a discrepancy in definitions of national interest. Many Japanese insist that if only Americans recognized the precarious nature of their agriculture and its importance to the Japanese way of life (the more so, in the face of arbitrary foreign actions such as the U.S. soybean embargo in the early 1970s), then the United States would not press so adamantly for greater market access for U.S. beef and citrus products. We insist, with equal vigor and self-righteousness, that if the Japanese took proper note of both U.S. economic ills and the interests of their own consumers, and if they gave appropriate consideration to the political impact on the thinking of members of the U.S. Congress of the continuing massive bilateral trade imbalance, then obviously they would respond favorably to our importunings.

Failure to acknowledge the existence of those divergent definitions, and hiding instead behind a facade of "misunderstanding," is as comfortable as it is self-serving. In its avoidance of reality, it is also dangerous.

For the U.S.-Japan partnership to reach anything close to its full potential (and remember that together they are responsible for nearly one-third of the gross global product every day), they must engage in a much more realistic and candid dialogue about the nature of their fundamental interests. To what extent are they shared, or at least compatible? Can the two countries, for example, come to a mutually acceptable definition of the Soviet threat? And if that proves possible, can they agree on what to do about it, individually and in tandem? Can they find ways to cooperate constructively in the economic sphere, fashioning general agreement on what is best for them, separately and jointly? Can they shape common approaches to third world development that will permit their very substantial capabilities to benefit those most in need?

Even nearing that level of understanding with its closest friends in Europe has been difficult for the United States, and in some areas beyond its reach. Where it has succeeded, its efforts have been assisted enormously by shared historical and cultural tradition. The challenge of approaching such a level between Japan and the United States, where such traditions do not exist, is infinitely greater. It is also supremely important.

Japan: "Visible Products, Invisible Leaders"

In spite of the burgeoning American interest in Japan, it is accurate to say that this nation of islands across the Pacific remains a considerable mystery to many Americans. There is, as we have seen, enormous respect for Japanese products and considerable warmth for the Japanese people — even if this has been diluted a bit in recent times.

Awareness of things Japanese, especially such visible products as cameras, watches, calculators, television sets, and the like, has brought Japan to the attention of virtually every American, to an extent that would have seemed almost unthinkable even a decade or so ago. The fascination in the United States with Japan and its people was manifested dramatically when a special television adaptation of the novel *Shogun* held tens of millions of Americans glued to their T.V. screens night after night. Whatever the merits of the production (and many questioned its accuracy and steadfastness to historical reality), the very fact that it commanded such huge audiences is testimony to the remarkable thirst that so many Americans have to learn more about this strange and marvelous land.

But when we looked at those Japanese attributes that Americans first think of as either most positive or most negative, the focus on things related to the economic arena, and to goods and products, is striking. There is, one might say, a certain mechanistic quality to Japan and the Japanese as they come across to Americans.

To put it another way, for many Americans Japan is the country of "visible products and invisible leaders." (Mr. Nakasone tried to alter that image, but as the oft-cited Japanese proverb puts it, "the nail that sticks up gets knocked down.") Americans, as just noted, are well aware of the extraordinary entry of Japan into the American marketplace—but they still have little idea of what the Japanese people, and especially their leaders, are all about. That can lead to a warped view, with Japan seen as powerful (more so than the situation warrants, in the Japanese view of themselves), immensely competent, but also threatening economically and playing by its own rules (the "economic animal" label).

Without a clearer sense of Japanese aims and purposes—a sense that needs first of all to be spelled out directly to Americans by Japanese leaders—Americans can become nervous and resentful about the Japanese challenge (just as Japanese can become nervous and resentful about unremitting American criticism and pressure).

Lack of Consultation and Continuity

From the Japanese standpoint, perhaps nothing is more troubling than what is seen as recurring spasms of American inconstancy and unreliability. Each incoming administration in Washington seems compelled to go through a period of reinventing many elements of U.S. foreign policy, leaving countries with close and important ties to the United States—Japan near the head of the list—uncertain what will come next.

Furthermore, and doubly irritating because it flies in the face of protestations to the contrary, American administrations are seen as wanting to share burdens without sharing decisionmaking. U.S. failure to consult with the Japanese leadership before opening ties with the People's Republic of China (one of the so-called "Nixon shocks" that remains a conversation staple in Tokyo) was a factor that helped cause the incumbent Japanese government to fall. More recently, the decision by the Reagan Administration to lift the wheat embargo on the Soviet Union without consulting with Japan—after Japan had endorsed American sanctions against the Soviet Union for invading Afghanistan—sent another round of shock waves through the Japanese body politic.

For the Japanese, predictability, constancy, and reliability are traits to be admired and cultivated. They find it difficult to cope with the policy zigzags and lurches of the country with whom their economic and security well-being is most closely linked. They expect better.

Differing Time Spectrums

Japanese and Americans tend to work on the basis of differing time spectrums. Japanese are more comfortable thinking in terms of decades when Americans talk of years. The American desire to find quick solutions contrasts with the Japanese emphasis on process and continuity.

This shows itself as well in the differing perspectives held by managers in the two countries, touched upon earlier. The American focus tends to be on the "bottom line," while Japanese management is content with lower profits at the expense of increased market share—a view that looks to long-term advantage rather than quick profit.

These are culturally induced mindsets that lead to divergent approaches to ongoing policy negotiations, with Japanese interlocutors frequently calling for patience and an extended timetable in addressing specific problem areas. From the American side, this can be seen as foot-dragging, giving rise to impatience and irritation.

Problems in Communicating

Tales of misunderstanding between Japanese and Americans, in both social and official settings, are legion. Their frequency—and at times their humor—does not lessen the problems, sometimes serious, that such misunderstandings can cause.

By most standards, Japanese is a difficult language. It is also one that very few Americans even try to learn, unlike the focus in Japan on learning English. One of the results of this one-sided language competence is that translations can come up with sets of words that mean very different things in the two tongues, without either side recognizing that fact.

The example noted most frequently is the Japanese mannerism of responding in conversation with a series of nods of the head and recurrent *hai's*, often taken by a visitor to mean "yes, I agree with you." When it turns out that the Japanese individual meant only "I hear you," that can lead to frustration and even feeling misled, however unwarranted.

Even subtler are the cases where word-for-word translations, although technically accurate, result in contrasting and even contradictory meanings in the two languages. Both English and Japanese, for example, contain the concept of "thinking in parallel." The connotations, however, are quite different. In English, to say "we are thinking along parallel lines" carries the connotation that our ideas are "in synch," that our thought processes are in tune, and that we are probably nearing agreement. In Japanese, to be thinking "in parallel" is accepted literally; like railroad tracks, the process goes on side by side, but never joins. Thus, agreement or joint understanding is out of the question.

Another example can be found in the idea of "a forward-looking response" or handling an issue "in a forward-looking manner." For most Americans, the implication is positive and constructive: "let's try to work something out," or "we'll consider this carefully and come back with something you can probably accept." Not so in Japan. There both parties understand that they are deadlocked and that it's time to put off the topic; agreement is beyond reach.

One must be careful, then, about assuming that words, concepts, and phrases mean the same thing just because they come out the same way in English. Pitfalls abound.

Unbalanced Levels of Awareness

Several references have been made to the far greater level of English-language proficiency in Japan than Japanese-language proficiency in the United States. That reflects a much larger imbalance—relative awareness in each country about the other.

However much Japanese influence may be growing in the United States, it is nothing compared to the American presence in Japan. That is extensive and everywhere, or at least almost everywhere. Perhaps it is most pervasive in the Japanese mass media. The amount of coverage given to actions by the American government, statements by influential (and frequently not-so-influential) figures, and events in the United States is enormous. Television news programs give such material top billing almost as a matter of course. Radio does the same. The major dailies feature massive coverage of the American scene. While the quality of all this material can vary extensively, the important fact is that the average Japanese citizen is exposed daily to a huge amount of information about the United States.

Nothing like this appears in the United States. Although the space and time allocated to Japan and things Japanese is increasing, it is still minor overall. On the American national scene, Japan competes with a host of other claimants. It does moderately well, at best.

For Japan, the United States looms large indeed. It is well to remember that many critical and sometimes ill-tempered statements by relatively unimportant Americans can be picked up by the Japanese media as something close to official U.S. government policy statements. Because of the at times random nature of Japanese media coverage and attention, the picture that comes through is frequently skewed.

Looked at from the broadest perspective, this imbalance has important ramifications. American awareness of current events and developments in Japan tends to be superficial and skimpy. The Japanese, on the other hand, with their vastly greater flow of information, tend to be far better informed about doings in the United States—and are regularly surprised at and bemused by (perhaps condescendingly insulted by would be a more accurate, if less diplomatic, way of putting it) the shallow knowledge shown by supposedly well-informed Americans.

Competition and Threat

One very strong element of U.S.-Japan ties today is a high degree of competitiveness. Not only is the competition fierce, it is centered on those areas of high technology formerly a private American preserve. As an economy, Japan is moving out of the sectors where its competitive advantage is small (shipbuilding, steel, and textiles, for example), into those where it can assume the lead. Japan is rapidly becoming a supplier of technology and capital, both intellectual and financial, that pits it directly against the United States.

There are at least two negative spinoffs from this newly competitive situation. First, as survey data have made clear, Americans are strongly of the view that Japan represents the principal foreign threat to the jobs of American workers. Japan is given this distinction by a margin of better than two-to-one over its closest rival, Taiwan. What has been one of Japan's greatest appeals—its high quality products, available at reasonable prices, and found to be superbly reliable—has developed a negative side. In a period of American economic travail, these highly visible goods, entering the U.S. market in large volume, have triggered fears among Americans over the impact on domestic economic health. This is not to say that Americans don't want these products. They do. But they also have reservations about the people who make make them, and what their remarkable industrial prowess is doing to us.

Second, we must not overlook the possibility that this competition, which shows no signs of abating, will bring the United States and Japan increasingly into conflict not only for markets for finished products, something already happening globally in the computer/electronics field, but are also for the same raw materials and natural resources to feed productive capacity. To the extent that such competition emerges more forcefully, one can expect that the cries of anguish and demands for protection already heard on Capitol Hill will become shriller and more insistent.

Differences in the Decision-Making Process

Just as there can be misunderstanding the meaning of words, so there can there be misunderstanding the way the other partner makes decisions.

Much is made of Japanese adherence to *ringi*—decisions made by consensus. This is not some kind of re-creation of the American Indian powwow or the primitive palaver. Rather, the Japanese, over centuries of relative confinement and endowed with internal homogeneity, have developed a tradition of moving deliberately and carefully toward important decisions, trying to make sure that all sides of the question at hand are addressed and that various views are heard. Then and only then—in theory at least—is the decision made. The process can take a long time, depending on the subject. That slowness is often interpreted by outside observers as another example of Japanese foot-dragging and playing for special advantage.

Having once been made on a consensus basis, however, the decision normally sticks. Furthermore, it can be implemented with a speed that can startle outside observers. Such has regularly been the case when Japanese companies move from prototypes to mass production with a haste and efficiency that leaves their competitors stunned and often crying "foul."

This contrasts sharply with American practice. The American idealization of being decisive and "tough" has fostered a tendency to want decisions to be reached quickly and often alone at the top. How often do we read about the solitary executive—up to and including the president in the White House—sitting alone late at night and coming single-handedly to conclusions that will affect all those below.

That process, perhaps overstated but still considered to be very "American," often leaves behind those below. Commitments made by chief executives don't stick. At the federal level, Congress intervenes to undo what presidents promised to deliver. The action that emerges from a presidential statement or policy speech can so vary from the original proposition as to be all but unrecognizeable. This can also leave outside observers nonplussed, but for quite different reasons than the Japanese example just cited.

It should be emphasized here that the question remains open on which approach is "better." The Japanese style includes within it a regimentation and final acceptance that smacks of authoritarianism. The American style includes within it checks and balances that have played a prominent and important role in U.S. history.

In the end, however, the approaches are different. As with the language problem, they open the door to frustration on both sides, and charges of double-dealing.

Legalism vs. Trust

American concern for putting things down in writing, and concluding detailed contracts, contrasts with Japanese emphasis on trust, and the assurance that one's word guarantees that the job will be done.

These are factors that flow once again from cultural and historical tradition, stemming in part from American heterogeneity and Japanese homogeneity. They can lead to actions that are hardly understandable when seen from the other side of the Pacific.

Take, for example, what happened in the aftermath of the crash of a Japan Air Lines jet at Haneda Airport in Tokyo in 1982, at the end of a flight from Fukuoka. The pilot, subsequently found to be mentally deranged, had exercised wild maneuvers during the approach that resulted in the death of a number of passengers. Following this tragedy, the chairman of the board of JAL personally visited the homes of families of the victims to express his sorrow and to make a modest bereavement payment on behalf of the airlines. For the persons involved, that brought the matter officially to a close.

It is, of course, impossible to imagine this scenario occurring in the United States. Such an action by a company official, especially the most senior representative, would have constituted acknowledgement of guilt and thereby virtually guaranteed a huge and favorable monetary settlement, either in court or out.

We protect ourselves and our individual claims in ways quite different. Japanese allow a greater element of what Americans look upon as paternalism than Americans have ever shown themselves willing to accept.

The Unfinished Security Debate

In all the controversy surrounding Japan's appropriate security role, and what should be its share of defense of the home islands and nearby territorial waters, one potentially divisive fact is either overlooked or not even recognized to exist.

Japan, by turning over its security to another power, from whom it is separated by a vast expanse of water, has done what few great powers in history have ever been willing to do—cede a meaningful portion of sovereignty, inherent in the right to full self-defense.

This is far different than the case in Europe, for example, where nations allied to the United States have undertaken substantial defense programs. Indeed, those programs have been a prerequisite for the continuing American nuclear umbrella and local stationing of U.S. ground troops. In Japan, on the other hand, such programs have been sharply limited—as dictated originally by America during the postwar occupation.

This is not to bring up again the "free ride" controversy; that has been discussed elsewhere. But it is to introduce a psychological consideration that deserves some careful thought.

We have seen declining confidence among Japanese in the commitment of the United States to come to Japan's defense if attacked. To be sure, this loss of confidence has not been matched by any widespread support for a markedly increased defense budget or enlarged Self Defense Forces. Nor has it evoked much sentiment in favor of a defense capability independent of the United States.

Yet it seems reasonable to speculate on whether this uneasiness represents ambivalence of greater or lesser degree. May not this limitation on traditional sovereignty impose a larger psychological burden than is generally acknowledged to be the case?

To be sure, that uneasiness could logically have been sublimated during earlier postwar years when the United States was seen as omnipotent and reliable. But that assessment of the United States, as we have seen, no longer applies.

In examining some of the generational shifts in Japanese thinking, we noticed a less supportive view among younger Japanese on policy issues of importance to the U.S. side, as well as growth of an attitude tinged with condescension and lessened confidence in America's reliability as an ally. Should that frame of mind persist, and become linked with some degree of frustration—or worse—over a perceived infringement on sovereignty, the result could be damaging indeed to the future of Japanese-American ties.

Learning How to Disagree

One of the encouraging signs found in the surveys has been agreement in public opinion when one might logically have expected the opposite. The apparent willingness of both Americans and Japanese to accept a meaningful share of the burden in some of the most vexatious areas of dispute—particularly in economic matters—gives hope for flexibility in negotiating compromise. As one example, in looking at American and Japanese views on whether the United States or Japan is rated more positively on such factors as easy market access or limited tariff barriers, one can argue that the Japanese people, in their overall agreement with Americans, have moved out in front of their leaders.

But there are, as we have also seen, substantial areas of disagreement. And the problem is compounded by the fact that as nations and competing partners we have not yet learned *how* to disagree. Disagreement without rancor between nations is possible, as in a good marriage, when there is a depth of common understanding, trust, and friendship that allows the partners to move constructively beyond the area of immediate discord. This is not yet a full characteristic of ties between the United States and Japan.

Consider, by way of contrast, relations between the United States and France. It seems as if there is almost always something at work to strain those bilateral ties. And yet there is also at work another something—an empathy based on culture, history, extensive personal and official interchange, schooling, and many other factors—that causes Americans, at least, to say "ah, but they are the French!" There is a built-in willingness, in other words, to explain away, if not completely forgive. Under such circumstances, disagreements are less tense and easier to paper over, even if not completely resolve.

Development of this ability to disagree amicably takes great time and patience. It is an element often lacking in the U.S.-Japan bilateral relationship. Many Japanese acknowledge that lack, but find free-swinging discussions, filled with sharp debate, extremely difficult to handle—more so, certainly, than do Americans. There have been encouraging signs of late that more spirited give-and-take is entering the dialogue. To the extent that both sides can become better able to handle disagreements, the partnership undoubtedly will benefit.

8 A LOOK TO THE FUTURE

The relationship between two great countries and talented peoples is both remarkably strong and yet weak. To the extent that we are content with the former and ignore or fail to recognize the latter, we are headed for ever more contentious and difficult times. That does not have to be, but it could come to pass.

A NEW REALISM?

One encouraging factor, touched upon in Chapter 2, is the appearance in 1983 of a firming up in at least some attitudes in each country toward the other. It is too early to tell whether this will be a lasting trend or just a short-term improvement. Perhaps an optimist can be forgiven, however, for hoping that this does, in fact, mark a settling down of views on both sides of the Pacific—a settling down brought about by a recognition on the part of concerned citizens in Japan and the United States that the relationship is too important to be frittered away. Such awareness, accompanied by efforts on both sides, individually and collectively, to improve matters, hold the prospect of breaking the down cycle both countries have been living through. But such an outcome is by no means guaranteed.

JAPAN: SEARCH FOR ALTERNATIVES?

The fundamental importance that Japan and the United States hold for each other, most obviously in economic and security terms but in other areas as well, has been remarked upon on numerous occasions throughout these pages. The truth of that assertion has tended to be taken for granted—and with that assumption another has followed, which goes something like this. No matter how touchy our relations get, they cannot fully break down because Japan does not have any place to go. Japan's economic well-being and physical security are so dependent upon the United States that Japanese policy will have to adjust to American pressures.

To the extent that this assumption is made—and by a number of observers and policy makers it is—we are entering into very dangerous waters. Almost nothing could feed the Japanese sense of insularity more than the conviction that this is the American view, and that Japan is losing an important element of its own birthright.

Among other things, it must be remembered that Japan *does* have alternatives. While a rush to accomodation with the Soviet Union does appear unlikely for the foreseeable future—in considerable measure because Soviet policy toward Japan is so inept, as if designed to alienate Japan and keep it bound to the United States—Japan's overseas relations show increasing signs of flexibility and willingness to dilute the intense U.S.-Japan bilateralism that has marked the entire postwar era.

One measure of this modest shift has been the steady expansion of links between Japan and its neighbors to the south—especially the ASEAN states (Indonesia, Malaysia, the Philippines, Singapore, and Thailand) and, more recently, Australia as well. In the face of the drawdown of U.S. strength in the Pacific as a result of the Nixon Doctrine and the American defeat in Vietnam, Japan has moved cautiously to fill some of that void, through a program of increased investment and aid, as well as regular diplomatic forays through the region by a succession of Japanese prime ministers.

Something like 70 percent of Japanese overseas development assistance and aid remains in Asia, with Indonesia an especially important recipient. A large portion of Japanese overseas manufacturing and labor investment is also placed in Asia. Japan is the principal market for many nations in the area. The Malaysian government has gone so far as to adopt a policy of "look East"—a catch phrase that calls for learning from and, to the extent appropriate, emulating the Japanese model.

Finally, it can only be taken as further evidence of Japanese interest in playing a larger diplomatic role in Asia that Prime Minister Nakasone, during a swing through the ASEAN countries and Brunei on the eve of the May 1983 Williamsburg Summit, offered to press ASEAN points of view and act as an ASEAN spokesman at that gathering of world leaders.

These are important straws in the wind. They are contributing to the realignment of U.S.-Japan links with which these pages began. They do represent other avenues for Japan—not a rejection of its ties with the United States, but most definitely other very powerful and effective arrows in its quiver.

It clearly behooves American leadership to recognize and understand the consequences of Japan's new assertiveness, a posture that can be a major force for stability and growth in the Asian region. But this assertion is also likely to put the United States and Japan into greater competition both there and elsewhere. That is a development that contains within it additional seeds of future discord, with the potential for damage touched upon in the previous chapter.

"WHO LOST JAPAN?" "WHO LOST AMERICA?"

In bringing these pages to a close, it is hard not to wonder and worry over what Japan and America are doing to each other, and why. The United States and Japan have so much to offer each other, so much to gain from close and mutually supportive ties, and so much to contribute globally, that it is tempting to think that they must be collectively losing their senses. Why else would they behave in many ways so selfishly, and pursue policies that seem preordained to aggravate an already inflamed situation?

There are, as we have seen, many imbalances in the U.S.-Japan equation—in trade, defense responsibilities, levels of confidence, and the like. In the final analysis, there is another imbalance that deserves mention here—the complaint and demand balance.

On this subject, most careful and close observers of the Japan-U.S. scene would say that it is the United States that leads. Leads, that is, in complaints and demands. Most Japanese complaints, in fact, are responses to our demands, while their own demands are considerably more circumspect. Japan has, furthermore, undertaken a wide variety of steps in response to foreign complaints, not always fully appreciated.

I do not mean this book to be simply an apologia for Japan. There can be no doubt that for many years Japan did maintain a highly protected market. It has used all kinds of bureaucratic and regulatory ploys to make things difficult for foreigners to do business. It has moved more slowly than is appropriate in accepting the political and security responsibilities that go hand in hand with its global economic power and reach. And it has engaged in economic practices that have at times brought considerable opprobrium.

As usual, though, there is another side to the coin. The United States has engaged, and continues to engage, in a number of activities that amount to protectionism or market restriction in one form or another. And many of the areas of discord with Japan have been either caused or exacerbated by poor U.S. management practices, short-sighted governmental policies and legislation, and a decline in excellence, whether in production or in service. Where those issues are concerned, it does little good to complain to or about others. The best remedy is to double one's own efforts to get things back on track. In some areas, what Japan has been able to accomplish should be admired and accepted as a challenge from which the United States can benefit. It still has, after all, a population twice the size of Japan's, and natural resources far in excess of Japan's wildest dreams.

When all is said and done, the Japanese are increasingly coming to the conclusion that they can never fully satisfy U.S. demands. As soon as one issue is addressed and at least partially resolved, another is rushed out to replace it. Not only that, but the demands and complaints have a way of escalating, with American political figures at times appearing to suggest that Japan must revise its own social rules of behavior—an intrusion that, if turned against the United States, would elicit the most heated rebuttal. By putting forth such demands, which are seen as excessive and unrealistic, America runs the risk of causing the Japanese simply to shrug their shoulders and walk away, convinced that we do not really mean what we say.

One is reminded, in the midst of the storm and controversy that now surround U.S.-Japan dealings, of similar recriminations of an earlier era—the bitterness, the endless name-calling, and the political poisoning that accompanied the feverish (if misguided) U.S. debate in the 1950s over "who lost China?"

The United States may, indeed, be approaching another such historical crossroads in the relationship between the United States and Japan. Can Japanese and Americans alike take the correct road—moving to cool the rhetoric, opening fully and strengthening the lines of communication, and working together to apply enormous capabilities more effectively to the good of both peoples and of all humankind?

How much better to follow that path than to face possible future anguishing over "who lost Japan?" or "who lost America?"

APPENDIX

METHODOLOGY

Most of the public opinion surveys referred to in this book were conducted by The Gallup Organization of Princeton, New Jersey or its Japanese affiliate, The Nippon Research Center of Tokyo. Especially important were directly comparable studies conducted in the United States and Japan in April 1982 and August 1983, as well as an earlier study conducted in the United States alone in June 1980. These included personal interviews with approximately 1500 adults 18 years of age and older in each country. Other surveys have been drawn upon as well, and are so indicated in the text.

DESIGN OF THE SAMPLE

The design of the sample used by The Gallup Organization is that of a replicated probability sample down to the block level in the case of urban areas and to segments of townships in the case of rural areas.

After stratifying the nation geographically and by size of community in order to insure conformity of the sample with the latest available estimates by the Census Bureau of the adult population, approximately

350 different sampling locations or areas (Census Tracts or Census Enumeration Districts) are selected on a mathematically random basis from within cities, counties, and towns which in turn have been selected on a mathematically random basis. The interviewers have no choice whasoever concerning the part of the city, town, or county in which they conduct their interviews.

Approximately five interviews are conducted in each such randomly selected sampling point. Interviewers are given maps of the area to which they are assigned, with a starting point indicated; they are required to follow a specified direction. At each occupied dwelling unit, interviewers are instructed to select respondents by following a pre-scribed systematic method and by a male-female assignment. This procedure is followed until the assigned number of interviews has been completed. Interviewing is conducted at times when adults in general are most likely to be at home—on weekends and weekdays after 4:00 p.m. for women and 6:00 p.m. for men.

SAMPLING ERROR

In interpreting survey results, it should be remembered that all sample surveys are subject to sampling error—that is, the extent to which the results may differ from what would be obtained if the whole population had been interviewed. The size of such sampling errors depends largely on the number of interviews. In the case of a sample of approximately 1500 (as used in most of the surveys referred to in these pages), the margin of error is plus or minus two to three percent. Differences between surveys, or trends over time, are judged significant and worthy of comment if such differences or shifts far exceed that given margin of error.

SIZE OF THE SAMPLE

The following table provides the approximate number of persons inter-viewed in each group for any single survey.

NATIONAL	1500
Sex	
Male	750
Female	750
Race	
White	1295
Total non-white	205
Blacks	180
Education	
College	540
High school	805
Grade school	155
Region	
East	415
Midwest	400
South	415
West	270
Age	
Total under 30	380
18-24 years	215
25-29 years	165
30-49 years	515
Total 50 & older	605
50-64	335
65 & older	270
Income	
$25,000 & over	465
$20,000-24,999	160
$15,000-19,999	230
$10,000-14,999	265
$5,000-9,999	245
Under $5,000	135
Politics	
Republican	410
Democrat	685
Independent	405
Occupation	
Professional and business	475
Clerical & sales	115
Manual workers	605
Skilled	275
Unskilled	330

NATIONAL	1500
Farmers	55
Non-labor force	250
City Size	
1,000,000 & over*	300
500,000-999,999*	195
50,000-499,999*	385
2,500-49,999	215
Under 2,500, rural	405

*Including urbanized areas around the central city.

INDEX

115

About the Author

William Watts is president of Potomac Associates and a consultant for The Gallup Organization. He also is a professorial lecturer at The Johns Hopkins University School of Advanced International Studies. He has served in the U.S. Foreign Service in Seoul and Moscow, and in the State Department's Office of Asian Communist Affairs and Bureau of Intelligence and Research, Soviet Affairs. He received the M.A. in Russian studies from Harvard University. He is the author or coauthor of numerous articles and books, including *State of the Nation III, Japan, Korea, and China: American Perceptions and Policies, The United States and China: American Perceptions and Future Alternatives, The United States and Korea: American Attitudes and Policies, The United States and Japan: American Perceptions and Policies, The United States and Korea: New Directions for the '80s,* and *The United States and Asia: Changing Attitudes and Policies.*